The Unfinished Revolution
Russia   1917–1967

ISAAC DEUTSCHER

The Unfinished Revolution
RUSSIA 1917-1967

The George Macaulay Trevelyan Lectures
delivered in the University of Cambridge
January–March 1967

London
OXFORD UNIVERSITY PRESS
New York   1967   Toronto

Oxford University Press, Ely House, London W. 1

Glasgow   New York   Toronto   Melbourne   Wellington
Cape Town   Salisbury   Ibadan   Nairobi   Lusaka   Addis Ababa
Bombay   Calcutta   Madras   Karachi   Lahore   Dacca
Kuala Lumpur   Hong Kong   Tokyo

Set in the United States of America
and printed lithographically in Great Britain
by Billing & Sons Ltd, Guildford and London

Acknowledgments

These Lectures are published here as they were delivered in the University of Cambridge in January–March 1967. I cherish the memory of the warmhearted response with which I met in the University from extraordinarily attentive audiences, from the Electors of the Trevelyan Lecturer, and in particular from the Master of Peterhouse, and the Master, Vice-Master, and Fellows of Christ's College.

I am indebted to my wife for ideas on how to deal within the compass of these six lectures with the great and complex problems of half a century of Soviet history. She has helped me to bring clarity into the difficult composition of this survey; such faults as readers will undoubtedly detect are entirely my own. I am grateful to my friend Professor E. F. C. Ludowyk for the critical understanding and patience with which he read the manuscript; and my thanks are due to Mr. John Bell and Mr. Dan M. Davin for their helpful suggestions for improvements.

London   I.D.
March 1967

Contents

The Unfinished Revolution
Russia   1917–1967

I

The Historical Perspective

What is the significance of the Russian revolution for our generation and age? Has the revolution fulfilled the hopes it aroused or has it failed to do so? It is natural that these questions should be asked anew now that half a century has passed since the fall of Tsardom and the establishment of the first Soviet government. The distance which separates us from these events seems long enough to yield a historical perspective. Even so, the distance may well be too short. This has been the most crowded and cataclysmic epoch in modern history. The Russian revolution has raised issues far deeper, has stirred conflicts more violent, and has unleashed forces far larger than those that had been involved in the greatest social upheavals of the past. And yet the revolution has by no means come to a close. It is still on the move. It may still surprise us by its sharp and sudden turns. It is still capable of re-drawing its own perspective. The ground we are entering is one which historians either fear to tread or must tread with fear.

To begin with, there is the fact, which we all take for granted, that the men who at present rule the Soviet Union describe themselves as the legitimate descendants of the Bolshevik Party of 1917. Yet this circumstance should hardly be taken for granted. There is no precedent for it in any of the modern revolutions that bear comparison with the upheaval in Russia. None of them lasted half a century. None of them maintained a comparable continuity, however relative, in political institutions, economic policies, legislative acts, and ideological traditions. Think only of the aspect England presented about fifty years after the execution of Charles I. By that time the English people, having lived under the Commonwealth, the Protectorate, and the Restoration, and having left the Glorious Revolution behind them, were trying, under the rule of William and Mary, to sort out, and even to forget, all this rich and stormy experience. And in the fifty years that followed the destruction of the Bastille, the French overthrew their old monarchy, lived under the Jacobin Republic, the Thermidor, the Consulate, and the Empire; saw the return of the Bourbons and overthrew them once again to put Louis Philippe on the throne, whose bourgeois kingdom had, by the end of the 1830s, used up exactly half of its lease on life—the revolution of 1848 was already looming ahead.

By its sheer duration the Russian revolution seems to make impossible the repetition of anything like this classical historical cycle. It is inconceivable that Russia should ever call back the Romanovs, even if only to overthrow them for a second time. Nor can we imagine the Russian landed aristocracy coming back, as the French came under the Restoration, to claim the estates, or compensation for the estates, of which they had been dispossessed. The great French landlords had been in exile only twenty years or so; yet the country to which they returned was so changed that they were strangers in it and could not recapture their past glories. The Russian landlords and capitalists who went into exile after 1917 have died out; and surely by now their children and grandchildren must have parted with their ancestral possessions even in their dreams. The factories and mines their parents or grandfathers once owned are a tiny fraction of the Soviet industry that has since been founded and developed under public ownership. The revolution seems to have outlasted all possible agents of restoration. Not only the parties of the *ancien régime* but also the Mensheviks and Social Revolutionaries, who dominated the political stage between February and October of 1917, have long ceased to exist even in exile, even as shadows of themselves. Only the party that gained victory in the October insurrection is still there in all its Protean power, ruling the country and flaunting the flag and the symbols of 1917.

But is it still the same party? Can we really speak of the revolution's continuity? Official Soviet ideologues claim that the continuity has never been broken. Others say that it has been preserved as an outward form only, as an ideological shell concealing realities that have nothing in common with the high aspirations of 1917. The truth seems to me more complex and ambiguous than these conflicting assertions suggest. But let us assume for a moment that the continuity is a mere appearance. We have still to ask what has caused the Soviet Union to cling to it so stubbornly? And how can an empty form, not sustained by any corresponding content, endure for so long? When successive Soviet leaders and rulers restate their allegiance to the original purposes and aims of the revolution, we cannot take their declarations at their face value; but neither can we dismiss them as wholly irrelevant.

Here again the historic precedents are instructive. In France at a similar remove from 1789 it would not have occurred to the men in office to present themselves as the descendants of Marat and Robespierre. France had nearly forgotten the great creative role that Jacobinism had played in her fortunes—she remembered Jacobinism only as the monster that had stood behind the guillotine in the days of the Terror. Only a few socialist doctrinaires, men like Buonarotti (himself a victim of the Terror), worked to rehabilitate the Jacobin tradition. England was long gripped by her revulsion against all that Cromwell and the Saints had stood for. G. M. Trevelyan, to whose noble historical work I here pay my respectful tribute, describes how this 'negative passion' swayed English minds even in the reign of Queen Anne.

Since the end of the Restoration, he says, the fear of Rome had revived; yet 'the events of fifty years back were responsible for an answering fear of Puritanism. The overthrow of the Church and of the aristocracy, the beheading of the King, and the rigid rule of the Saints had left a negative impression almost as formidable and permanent as the memory of "Bloody Mary" and James II.' The force of the anti-Puritan reaction showed itself, according to Trevelyan, in the fact that in the reign of Queen Anne 'The Cavalier and Anglican view of the Civil War held the field; the Whigs scoffed at it in private, but only occasionally dared to contradict it in public.'[1] True, Tory and Whig went on arguing about the 'revolution'; but the events they referred to were those of 1688 and 1689, not those of the 1640s. Two centuries had to pass before Englishmen began to change their view of the 'Great Rebellion' and to speak about it with more respect as a revolution; and even more time had to elapse before Cromwell's statue could be put up in front of the House of Commons.

The Russians are still daily flocking, in a mood of quasi-religious veneration, to Lenin's tomb at the Red Square. When they repudiated Stalin and ejected him from the Mausoleum, they did not tear his body to pieces as the English had torn Cromwell's and the French Marat's remains; they quietly reburied him under the Heroes' Wall at the Kremlin. And when his successors decided to disown part of his legacy, they professed to be going back to the revolution's spiritual fountainhead, to Lenin's principles and ideas. No doubt all this is part of a bizarre Oriental ritualism, but underneath there runs a powerful current of continuity. The heritage of the revolution survives in one form or another in the structure of society and in the nation's mind.

Time is, of course, relative even in history; half a century may mean a great deal or it may mean little. Continuity too is relative. It may be—indeed, it is—half real and half illusory. It is

[1] G. M. Trevelyan, *England under Queen Anne, Blenheim,* Chapter III.

solidly based yet it is brittle. It has its great blessings, but also its curses. In any case, within the framework of the revolution's continuity sharp breaks have occurred, which I hope to examine later. But the framework is massive enough; and no serious historian can gloss it over or remain uninfluenced by it in his approach to the revolution. He cannot view the events of this half-century as one of history's aberrations or as the product of the sinister design of a few evil men. What we have before us is a huge, throbbing piece of objective historic reality, an organic growth of man's social experience, a vast widening of the horizons of our age. I am, of course, referring mainly to the creative work of the October revolution, and I make no apologies for this. The February revolution of 1917 holds its place in history only as the prelude to October. People of my generation have seen several such 'February revolutions'; we saw them, in 1918, in countries other than Russia—in Germany, Austria, and Poland, when the Hohenzollerns and Habsburgs lost their thrones. But who will speak nowadays of the German revolution of 1918 as a major formative event of this century? It left intact the old social order and was a prelude only to the ascendancy of Nazism. If Russia had become similarly arrested in the February revolution and produced, in 1917 or 1918, a Russian variety of the Weimar Republic—what reason is there to assume that we should have remembered the Russian revolution to-day?

And yet quite a few theorists and historians still view the October revolution as an almost fortuitous event. Some argue that Russia might well have been spared the revolution if only the Tsar had been less obstinate in insisting on his absolute prerogatives and if he had come to terms with the loyal Liberal opposition. Others say that the Bolsheviks would never have had their chance if Russia had not become involved in the First World War or if she had withdrawn from it in time, before defeat reduced her to chaos and ruin. The Bolsheviks, according to this view, triumphed because of the errors and miscalculations committed by the Tsar and his advisers or by the men who took

office immediately after the Tsar's downfall; and we are asked to
believe that these errors and miscalculations were chance occurrences, accidents of individual judgment or decision. That the
Tsar and his advisers committed many foolish mistakes is, of
course, true. But they committed them under the pressure of the
Tsarist bureaucracy and of those elements in the possessing
classes who had a stake in the monarchy. Nor were the governments of the February regime, the governments of Prince Lvov
and Kerensky, free agents. They kept Russia in the war because,
like the Tsarist governments, they were dependent on those powerful Russian and foreign centres of finance-capital which were
determined that Russia should remain to the end a belligerent
member of the Entente. The 'errors and miscalculations' were
socially conditioned. It is also true that the war drastically exposed and aggravated the fatal weakness of the *ancien régime*.
But it was hardly the decisive cause of that weakness. Russia had
been shaken by the tremors of revolution just before the war; the
streets of St. Petersburg were covered with barricades in the summer of 1914. Indeed the outbreak of hostilities and the mobiliza-
tion swamped the incipient revolution and delayed it by two
years and a half, only to charge it eventually with greater explosive force. Even if Prince Lvov's or Kerensky's government had
contracted out of the war, it would have done so under conditions of a social crisis so profound and severe that the Bolshevik
Party would probably still have won, if not in 1917 then some
time later. This is, of course, only a hypothesis; but its plausibil-
ity is now reinforced by the fact that in China Mao Tse-tung's
party seized power in 1949, four years after the end of the Second
World War. This circumstance throws perhaps a restrospective
light on the connexion between the First World War and the
Russian revolution—it suggests that this connexion might not
have been as clear cut as it appeared at the time.

We need not assume that the course of the Russian revolution
was predetermined in all its features or in the sequence of all its
major phases and incidents. But its general direction had been

set not by the events of a few years or months; it had been prepared by the developments of many decades, indeed of several epochs. The historian who labours to reduce the mountain of the revolution to a few contingencies, stands as helpless before it as once stood the political leaders who sought to prevent its rise.

After every revolution its enemies question its historic legitimacy—sometimes they do so even two or three centuries later. Allow me to recall how Trevelyan answered the historians who still wondered whether the Great Rebellion was really necessary: 'Was it then impossible for Parliamentary power to take root in England at a less cost than this national schism and appeal to force . . . ? It is a question which no depth of research or speculation can resolve. Men were what they were, uninfluenced by the belated wisdom of posterity, and thus they acted. Whether or not any better way could have led to the same end, it was by the sword that Parliament actually won the right to survive as the dominant force of the English Constitution.'[2] Trevelyan, who follows here in Macaulay's footsteps, renders precise justice to the Great Rebellion, even while he underlines that it left the nation 'poorer and less noble' for a time, which is, unfortunately, in one sense or another true also of other revolutions, including the Russian. In stressing that England owed its parliamentary constitution primarily to the Great Rebellion, Trevelyan takes the long-term view of the role of the Puritans. It was Cromwell and the Saints, he says, who established the principle of Parliament's supremacy; and even though they themselves were in conflict with the principle and appeared to obliterate it, the principle survived and triumphed. The 'good deeds' of the Puritan revolution outlasted its follies.

Mutatis mutandis, the same may be said of the October revolution. 'Men acted as they did because they could not act otherwise.' They could not copy their ideals from Western European models of parliamentary democracy. It was by the sword that

[2] G. M. Trevelyan, A *Shortened History of England*, Book Four, Chapter II.

B

they won for the Councils of Workers' and Peasants' Deputies—
and for socialism—'the right to survive as the dominant force' in
the Soviet constitution. And although they themselves then reduced the Workers' Councils to a shadowy existence, those
Councils, the Soviets, and their socialist aspirations, have remained the most significant parts of the message of the Russian
revolution.

As for the French revolution, its necessity was questioned or
denied by a long line of thinkers and historians, from Burke, fear-
ful of the Jacobin contagion, to Tocqueville, distrustful of any
modern democracy, and Taine, horrified by the Commune of
Paris, down to Madelin, Bainville, and their disciples, some of
whom laboured after 1940, under Marshal Pétain's encouraging
gaze, to lay the ghost of the revolution. Curiously, of all those
writers Tocqueville has recently enjoyed the greatest vogue in
English-speaking countries. Quite a few of our learned men have
tried to model their conception of contemporary Russia on his
L'Ancien Régime et la Révolution. They are attracted by his argument that the revolution had made no radical departure from
the French political tradition, that it merely followed the basic
trends that had been at work under the *ancien régime*, especially
the trend towards the centralization of the State and the unification of national life. Similarly, the argument runs, the Soviet
Union, in so far as it has any progressive achievement to its
credit, has merely continued the work of industrialization and
reform that had been undertaken by the *ancien régime*. If Tsardom had survived, or if it had been replaced by a bourgeois democratic republic, that work would have gone on; and progress
would have been more orderly and rational. Russia might have
become the world's second industrial power without having to
pay the terrible price the Bolsheviks have exacted, without having to endure the expropriations, the terror, the low standards of
living, and the moral degradation of Stalinism.

It seems to me that Tocqueville's disciples do an injustice to
their master. Although he belittled the creative and original work

of the revolution, he did not deny its necessity or legitimacy. On the contrary, by placing it within the French tradition, he sought to 'adopt' it, on his own conservative terms, and to 'incorporate' it into the national heritage. His imitators show greater zeal for belittling the original and creative work of the Russian revolution than for 'adopting' it, on whatever terms. But let us consider the Tocquevillesque argument more closely. Of course, no revolution creates *ex nihilo*. Every revolution works in the social environment that has produced it and on the materials it finds in that environment. 'We are building a new order,' Lenin liked to say, 'out of the bricks the old order has left us.' Traditional methods of government, vital national aspirations, a style of life, habits of thought, and various accumulated factors of strength and weakness—these are the 'bricks.' The past refracts itself through the innovating work of the revolution, no matter how bold the innovations. The Jacobins and Napoleon continued indeed to build the unitary and centralized State that the *ancien régime* had up to a point promoted. No one emphasized this more forcefully than Karl Marx in his *18th Brumaire*, which appeared some years before Tocqueville's *Ancien Régime*. And it is equally true that Russia had made a real start in industrialization in the reign of the last two Tsars, without which the rapid entry of her industrial working class upon the political stage would not have been possible. Both countries thus achieved under the *ancien régime* some progress in various directions. This does not mean that the progress could go on in an 'orderly' manner, without the gigantic 'disturbance' of revolution. On the contrary, what was destroying the *ancien régime* was precisely the progress achieved under it. Far from making the revolution superfluous, it made it all the more necessary. The forces of progress were so constricted within the old order that they had to burst it. The French striving for the unitary State had been in chronic conflict with the barriers set to it by particularisms of feudal origin. France's growing bourgeois economy needed a single national market, a free peasantry, free movement of men and commodities; and the *ancien régime* could not satisfy these needs, except within the narrowest of limits. As a Marxist would put it: France's productive forces had outgrown her feudal property relations, and could no longer be contained within the shell of the Bourbon monarchy, which conserved and protected those relations.

In Russia the problem was similar but more complicated. The efforts made in Tsarist times to modernize the fabric of national life were blocked by the heavy residuum of feudalism, the underdevelopment and weakness of the bourgeoisie, the rigidity of the autocracy, the archaic system of government, and, last but not least, by Russia's economic dependence on foreign capital. The great Empire was, in the reign of the last Romanovs, half empire and half colony. Western shareholders owned 90 per cent of Russia's mines, 50 per cent of her chemical industry, over 40 per cent of her engineering plants, and 42 per cent of her banking stock. Domestic capital was scarce. The national income was far too small in relation to modern needs. More than half of it came from farming, which was utterly backward and contributed little to the accumulation of capital. Within limits the State provided, out of taxation, the sinews of industrialization—it built the railways, for instance. But in the main it was on foreign capital that industrial expansion depended. Foreign investors, however, had no continuous interest in ploughing back their high dividends into Russian industry, especially when the vagaries of a self-willed bureaucracy and social unrest deterred them. Russia could achieve the industrial 'take off,' to use Professor Rostow's term, only by drawing on the resources of her agriculture and through the extraordinary exertions of her own workers. None of these requirements could be fulfilled under the *ancien régime*. The Tsarist governments were too strongly dependent on Western finance-capital to assert Russia's national interests against it; and they were too feudal in their background and social connexions to release farming from the paralyzing grip of the landed aristocracy (from whose *milieu* came even the Prime Minister of the first republican government of 1917!). And none of the pre-Bolshevik governments had the political strength and moral authority to obtain from the working class the exertions and sacrifices that industrialization demanded in any circumstances. None had the outlook, the determination, and the modern mind that the task required. (Count Witte, with his ambitious schemes for reform, was the exception that confirmed the rule; and he, as Prime Minister and Minister of Finance, was almost boycotted by the Tsar and the bureaucracy.) It seems inconceivable that any regime not inherently revolutionary should have been able to raise a semi-illiterate peasant nation to anything approaching the present level of Soviet economic development and education. Here again, the Marxist will say that Russia's productive forces had advanced just far enough under the old regime to burst the old social structure and its political superstructure.

No automatic economic mechanism, however, produces the final disintegration of an old established order or assures the success of a revolution. An obsolete social system may be declining in the course of decades, and the bulk of the nation may be unaware of it. Social consciousness lags behind social being. The objective contradictions of the *ancien régime* have to translate themselves into subjective terms, into the ideas, aspirations, and passions of men in action. The essence of revolution, says Trotsky, is 'the direct intervention of the masses in historic events.' It is because of that intervention—a phenomenon so real and so rare in history—that the year 1917 was so remarkable and momentous. The great mass of the people were seized by the most intense and urgent awareness of decay and rot in the established order. The seizure was sudden. Consciousness leapt forward to catch up with being, and to change it. But this leap too, this sudden change in the psychology of the masses, did not come *ex nihilo*. It took many, many decades of revolutionary ferment and of a slow growth of ideas—it took the birth and the withering away of many parties and groups—to produce the moral-political climate, the leaders, the parties, and the methods of action of

1917. There was little or nothing fortuitous in all this. Behind this last half-century of revolution there loomed a whole century of revolutionary endeavour.

The social crisis under which Tsarist Russia laboured manifested itself in the stark contrast between her status and importance as a great power and the archaic weakness of her social structure, between the splendours of her empire and the wretchedness of her institutions. This contrast was laid bare for the first time by Russia's triumph in the Napoleonic wars. Her boldest spirits were aroused to action. In 1825 the Decembrists rose in arms against the Tsar. They were an aristocratic, intellectual elite; but they had the bulk of the nobility against them. No social class in Russia was capable of promoting the nation's progress. The towns were few and medieval in character; the urban middle classes, unlettered merchants and artisans, were politically negligible. The peasant-serfs rebelled sporadically; but since Pugachev's defeat there had been no large-scale action aiming at their emancipation. The Decembrists were revolutionaries without any revolutionary class behind them. This was their tragedy; and this was to be the tragedy of all successive generations of Russian radicals and revolutionaries almost till the end of the nineteenth century—in different forms the tragedy was to project itself into the post-revolutionary epoch as well.

Let me recapitulate briefly its main acts and motifs. Before the middle of the nineteenth century, new radicals and revolutionaries, the *Raznotchintsy*, made their appearance. They came from the slowly growing middle classes; many were children of civil servants and priests. They too were revolutionaries in search of a revolutionary class. The bourgeoisie was still negligible. The civil servants and priests were terrified of their rebellious sons. The peasantry was apathetic and passive. Only a section of the nobility favoured some reform, namely, the landlords who, eager to adopt modern methods of farming or to engage in industry and trade, wished to see serfdom abolished and the administration of the State and education liberalized. When Alexander II, yielding to their persuasion, abolished serfdom, he thereby secured for the dynasty the peasantry's unwavering allegiance for decades ahead. The 1861 Act of Emancipation thus isolated again the radicals and the revolutionaries and, in effect, postponed revolution by over half a century. Yet the land problem remained unresolved. The serfs had been freed, but had received no land; and they had to contract heavy debts and servitudes, and to become sharecroppers, in order to be able to till the land. The nation's way of life remained anachronistic. This state of affairs and the oppressiveness of the autocracy drove ever new men of the intelligentsia to revolt, to produce new ideas, and to experiment with ever new methods of political struggle.

Each successive group of revolutionaries drew its strength only from itself; for each an impasse waited at the end of its road. The *Narodniks* or Populists, inspired by Herzen and Bakunin, Chernyshevsky and Lavrov, were objectively the peasantry's militant vanguard. But when they appealed to the *muzhiks* and tried to open their eyes to the fraud of the emancipation and to the new manner in which the Tsar and the landlords kept them in subjection, the ex-serfs refused to budge or even to listen; not rarely they delivered the *Narodniks* into the hands of the gendarmes. An oppressed social class, with great revolutionary potentialities, thus betrayed its own revolutionary elite. The successors of the *Narodniks*, the *Narodnovoltsy*, abandoned the apparently hopeless search for a revolutionary popular force in society. They decided to act alone as the trustees of an oppressed and mute people. Their politically inspired terrorism took the place of the agrarian Populism of their predecessors. The propagandist or agitator of the previous era, who 'went out to the people' or even tried to settle among the peasants, was replaced by the lonely, taciturn, heroic conspirator, with the suggestion of a Superman, who, determined to vanquish or perish, took upon himself the task the nation was unable to accomplish. The circle whose members assassinated Alexander II in 1881 consisted of fewer than two score of men and women. Six years later only a

dozen young people, among them Lenin's elder brother, formed
the group that planned an attempt on the life of Alexander III.
These tiny conspiratorial bodies held the huge empire in sus-
pense, and made history. Yet, if the failure of the Populists of
the 1860s and 1870s had demonstrated the unreality of the hope
that the peasantry might be moved to rise, the martyrdom of
the *Narodnovoltsy* of the 1880s exposed once again the impotence of a vanguard which acted without the support of any of
the basic social classes. These negative experiences taught invalu-
able lessons to the revolutionaries of the next decades—and in
this sense they were not fruitless. The moral drawn by Plekhanov, Zasulich, Lenin, Martov, and their comrades was that
they must not act as an isolated vanguard, but must look for
support to a revolutionary class—and must look beyond the
peasantry. By now, however, the beginning of Russia's industrialization was solving the problem for them. The Marxist propagandists and agitators of Lenin's generation found their audience
among the new factory workers.

We should note the transparent dialectics of this protracted
struggle. There is first of all the contradiction between social
need and social consciousness. No social need or interest could
have been more elementary than the peasants' hunger for land
and freedom; and no social consciousness could have been more
false than the one that allowed them to content themselves, for
half a century, with an Act which, while freeing them from chat-
tel slavery, denied them land and freedom—a consciousness that
induced generations of *muzhiks* to hope that the Tsar-*Batiushka*
would right their wrongs. This discrepancy between need and
consciousness lay at the root of the many metamorphoses of the
revolutionary movement. The logic of the situation produced
these opposite models of organization: the self-sufficient conspiratorial elite on the one hand, and the mass-oriented movement on the other, the dictatorial and the democratic types of
the revolutionary. We should note also the special, exclusive,
and historically effective role that the intelligentsia played in all

this—in no other country do we find anything like it. Generation after generation, they stormed the Tsarist autocracy and smashed their heads against its walls, preparing the way for those who were to come after them. They were inspired by an almost Messianic faith in their, and in Russia's, revolutionary mission. When at last the Marxists came to the fore, they inherited a great tradition and a unique experience; they assessed both critically and used them effectively. But they also inherited certain problems and dilemmas.

The Marxists started out, as they had to, with the negation of the Populist and terrorist traditions. They rejected 'agrarian socialism,' the sentimental idealization of the peasantry, the radical versions of Slavophilism, and the quasi-Messianic idea of Russia's unique revolutionary mission. They repudiated terrorism, the self-glorification of the radical intellectual, and the self-sufficient conspiratorial elite. They opted for the democratically oriented organization, the party and the trade unions, and for modern forms of proletarian mass action. This attitude, 'strictly' or even exclusively proletarian and distrustful of the peasantry, was characteristic of the beginnings of the entire Russian Social Democratic Party; it was to remain typical of the Mensheviks in their best period. But the movement, as it passed to action, could not rest on the abstract negation of the native revolutionary traditions—it had to absorb what was vital in them and transcend them. It was Bolshevism that accomplished this task, and it did so long before 1917. The Bolsheviks inherited from the Populists their sensitivity towards the peasantry, and from the *Narodnovoltsy* their concentrated aggressiveness and their conspiratorial determination. Without these elements Marxism in Russia would have remained an exotic plant, or at best, a theoretical outgrowth of Western European socialism, as it was in Plekhanov's brilliant opus and in some of Lenin's youthful writings. The Russian acclimatization of Marxism was, above all, Lenin's achievement. He produced the synthesis of the doctrine with the native tradition. He insisted on the need for the workers, the

leading force in the revolution, to gain allies in the peasants; and
he assigned to the intellectuals and the revolutionary elite a
weighty, educative and organizing role in the workers' mass
movement. This synthesis epitomized the century of Russian
revolutionary endeavour.

If I were to stop here, I might give you a one-sided view of
the elements that went into the making of the revolution.
Though it is customary in the West to treat Bolshevism as a
purely Russian phenomenon, it is hardly possible to exaggerate
the contribution that Western Europe had made to it. Throughout the nineteenth century Russia's revolutionary thought and
action were, at every stage, decisively influenced by Western
ideas and movements. The Decembrists, belonged, no less than,
say, the *Carbonari*, to the European aftermath of the French
revolution. Many of them had been, after Napoleon's downfall,
young officers of the Russian occupation troops in Paris; and
contact even with the defeated revolution was enough to set
their minds ablaze. The *Petrashevtsy*, Belinsky and Herzen, Bakunin and Chernyshevsky, and so many others were formed by
the events of 1830 and 1848, by French socialism, German phi-
losophy, especially by Hegel and Feuerbach, and by British political economy. Then Marxism, itself embodying all these in-
fluences, made its stupendous intellectual conquest of radical
and even of liberal Russia. No wonder the apologists of Tsardom
denounced socialism and Marxism as products of the 'decadent'
West. Not only Pobedonostsev, the crude preacher of obscurant-
ism and Pan-Slavism, not only Dostoevsky, but even Tolstoy
repudiated the ideas of socialism in such terms. And they were
not quite mistaken: whether the West wishes to remember this
or not, it has invested a great deal of its own spiritual heritage in
the Russian revolution. Trotsky once wrote about the 'paradox,'
that while Western Europe 'exported its most advanced technology to the United States . . . it exported its most advanced
ideology to Russia. . . .' Lenin makes the same point, plainly
and forcefully: '. . . in the course of about half a century,

roughly from the 1840s till the 1890s, progressive thought in Russia searched avidly . . . for the correct revolutionary theory, and followed with remarkable zeal and meticulousness every "last word" that came from Europe and America. Russia has indeed come to Marxism . . . through extreme sufferings, ago-nies, and sacrifices . . . through learning, testing in practice . . . and engaging in a comparative study of Europe's experi-ence. Because Tsardom forced us to lead an émigré existence, revolutionary Russia . . . had at her command such a wealth of international contacts and so excellent an awareness of all the forms and theories of revolutionary movements all over the world as no one else possessed.'

In 1917 and in the following years not only the leaders but also the great mass of Russian workers and peasants saw the revolution not as the business of Russia alone, but as part of a social upheaval embracing the whole of mankind. The Bolshe-viks considered themselves the champions of at least a European revolution, whose battles they were waging on Europe's eastern outposts. Even the Mensheviks had held this conviction and had eloquently expressed it. And not only the Russians saw them-selves in this light. Early in this century Karl Kautsky, the lead-ing theorist of the Socialist International, drew this perspective: 'The epicentre of revolution has been moving from the West to the East. In the first half of the nineteenth century it was situ-ated in France, at times in England. In 1848 Germany entered the ranks of the revolutionary nations. . . . Now the Slavs . . . join their ranks, and the centre of gravity of revolutionary thought and action is more and more shifting . . . to Russia.' 'Russia, having taken over so much revolutionary initiative from the West, may now in her turn become a source of revolutionary energy for the West,' Kautsky remarked on the contrast with the situation in 1848, when the Peoples' Spring in Western Europe was nipped by the 'hard frost from Russia'; now the storm from Russia might help to clear the air in the West.

Kautsky wrote this in 1902 for *Iskra*, of which Lenin was co-editor; and his words made such an impression on Lenin that nearly twenty years later he quoted them with ironic delight against their author, now outraged by the fulfilment of his forecast. The forecast was in fact even more portentous than either Kautsky or Lenin perceived. We have seen how in our time the epicentre of revolution has shifted even farther to the East, from Russia to China. A historian with a flair for the grand generalization might extrapolate the perspective sketched by Kautsky and draw a more sweeping line, illustrating the eastward advance of the revolution in the course of three centuries. The line might start in Puritan England, traverse the whole of Europe, sweep on to China, and finally touch the south-eastern fringes of Asia.

However, such a graph may be misleading; it may suggest too linear and too strongly predetermined a course of history. But in whatever degree the course was determined or not, it has, clearly, had its inner coherence and logic. Goethe once said that the history of knowledge is a great fugue, in which the voices of the various nations appear one after another. One might say the same of the history of revolution. It is not the world symphony some of the great revolutionaries had hoped for. Nor is it the medley of discordant solos, the cacophony the Philistines hear. It is rather the great fugue in which the voices of the various nations, each with its own hopes and despairs, enter one after another.

II

Breaks in Revolutionary
Continuity

In 1917 Russia lived through the last of the great bourgeois revolutions and the first proletarian revolution in European history. The two revolutions merged into one. Their unprecedented coalescence imparted extraordinary vitality and *élan* to the new regime; but it was also the source of severe strains and stresses and cataclysmic convulsions.

I should perhaps give here, at the risk of stating the obvious, a brief definition of bourgeois revolution. The traditional view, widely accepted by Marxists and anti-Marxists alike, is that in such revolutions, in Western Europe, the bourgeoisie played the leading part, stood at the head of the insurgent people, and seized power. This view underlies many controversies among historians; the recent exchanges, for instance, between Professor Hugh Trevor-Roper and Mr. Christopher Hill on whether the Cromwellian revolution was or was not bourgeois in character. It seems to me that this conception, to whatever authorities it may be attributed, is schematic and historically unreal. From it one may well arrive at the conclusion that bourgeois revolution is almost a myth, and that it has hardly ever occurred, even in the West. Capitalist entrepreneurs, merchants, and bankers were not conspicuous among the leaders of the Puritans or the commanders of the Ironsides, in the Jacobin Club or at the head of the crowds that stormed the Bastille or invaded the Tuileries. Nor did they seize the reins of government during the revolution or for a long time afterwards, either in England or in France. The lower middle classes, the urban poor, the plebeians, and *sans culottes* made up the big insurgent battalions. The leaders were mostly 'gentlemen farmers' in England and lawyers, doctors, journalists, and other intellectuals in France. Here and there the upheavals ended in military dictatorship. Yet the bourgeois character of these revolutions will not appear at all mythical, if we approach them with a broader criterion and view their general impact on society. Their most substantial and enduring achievement was to sweep away the social and political institutions that had hindered the growth of bourgeois property and of the social relationships that went with it. When the Puritans denied the Crown the power of arbitrary taxation, when Cromwell secured for English shipowners a monopolistic position in England's trading with foreign countries, and when the Jacobins abolished feudal prerogatives and privileges, they created, often unknowingly, the conditions in which manufacturers, merchants, and bankers were bound to gain economic predominance and, in the long run, social and even political supremacy. Bourgeois revolution creates the conditions in which bourgeois property can flourish. In this, rather than in the particular alignments during the struggle, lies its *differentia specifica*.

It is in this sense that we can characterize the October revolution as a combination of bourgeois and proletarian revolutions, though both were accomplished under Bolshevik leadership. Current Soviet historiography describes the February revolution as bourgeois and reserves the label 'proletarian' for the October insurrection. This distinction is made by many Western historians too and is justified on the ground that in February, after the Tsar's abdication, the bourgeoisie seized power. In truth, the combination of the two revolutions had already appeared in February, but in a shadowy form. The Tsar and his last government were brought down by a general strike and a mass insurrection of workers and soldiers who at once created their Councils or Soviets, the potential organs of a new State. Prince Lvov, Miliukov, and Kerensky took power from the hands of a confused and groping Petrograd Soviet, which willingly yielded it to them; and they exercised it only for as long as the Soviets tolerated them. But their governments carried out no major act of bourgeois revolution. Above all, they did not break up the aristocracy's landed estates and give land to the peasants. Even as a bourgeois revolution, the February revolution was *manquée*.

All this underlines the prodigious contradiction with which the Bolsheviks undertook to cope when in October they promoted and directed the double upheaval. The bourgeois revolution over which they presided created conditions which favoured the growth of bourgeois forms of property. The proletarian revolution they accomplished aimed at the abolition of property. The main act of the former was the sharing out of the aristocracy's land. This created a wide potential base for the growth of a new rural bourgeoisie. The peasants who had been freed from rents and debts and had enlarged their farms were interested in a social system that would offer security to their holdings. Nor was this a matter only of capitalist farming. Rural Russia was, as Lenin put it, the breeding ground of capitalism at large—many of Russia's industrial entrepreneurs and merchants had been of peasant stock; and, given time and favourable circumstances, the peasantry might have bred a far more numerous and modern class of entrepreneurs. All the more ironic was it that in 1917 none of the bourgeois parties, not even the moderate Socialists, dared to sanction the agrarian revolution which was developing spontaneously, with elemental force, for the peasants were seizing the aristocracy's land long before the Bolshevik insurrection. Terrified by the dangers that threatened property in town, the bourgeois parties refused to undermine property in the country. The Bolsheviks (and the Left Social Revolutionaries) alone placed themselves at the head of the agrarian revolts. They

knew that without the upheaval in the country the proletarian
revolution would be isolated in town and defeated. The peasants,
afraid of a counter-revolution that might bring back the landlords, thus acquired a stake in the Bolshevik regime. But from
the outset the socialist aspects of the revolution aroused their
misgivings, fears, or hostility.

The socialist revolution was supported wholeheartedly by the
urban working class. But this was a small minority of the nation.
Altogether one-sixth of the population, twenty-odd million people, lived in the towns: and of these only half or so could be
described as proletarian. The hard core of the working class consisted at the most of about three million men and women employed in modern industry. Marxists had expected the industrial
workers to be the most dynamic force in capitalist society, the
main agents of socialist revolution. The Russian workers more
than justified this expectation. No class in Russian society, and
no working class anywhere in the world, has ever acted with the
energy, the political intelligence, the ability for organization, and
the heroism with which the Russian workers acted in 1917 (and
thereafter in the civil war). The circumstance that Russia's modern industry consisted of a small number of huge factories, concentrated mainly in Petrograd and Moscow, gave the massed
workers of the two capitals an extraordinary striking power at
the very nerve centres of the *ancien régime*. Two decades of intensive Marxist propaganda, fresh memories of the struggles of
1905, 1912, and 1914, the tradition of a century of revolutionary
endeavour, and Bolshevik singleness of purpose had prepared the
workers for their role. They took the socialist aim of the revolution for granted. They were not content with anything less than
the abolition of capitalist exploitation, socialization of industry
and banking, workers' control over production, and government
by Soviets. They turned their backs on the Mensheviks, whom
they had followed at first, because the Mensheviks were telling
them that Russia was not 'ripe for a socialist revolution.' Their
action, like that of the peasants, had its own spontaneous force:

they established their control over production at the factory level well before the October insurrection. The Bolsheviks supported them and turned the factory rebellions into a socialist revolution.

Yet Petrograd and Moscow, and a few other scattered industrial centres, constituted an extremely narrow base for this undertaking. Not only did people over the whole immensity of rural Russia scramble to acquire property while the workers of the two capitals strove to abolish it; not only was the socialist revolution in implicit conflict with the bourgeois one; in addition, it was fraught with its own inner contradictions. Russia was and was not ripe for socialist revolution. She was better able to cope with its negative than with its positive tasks. Guided by the Bolsheviks, the workers expropriated the capitalists and transferred power to the Soviets; but they could not establish a socialist economy and a socialist way of life; and they were unable to maintain their dominant political position for any length of time.

At first, the dual character of the revolution was, as has been said, the source of its strength. If a bourgeois revolution had taken place earlier (or if, at the time of the Emancipation, in 1861, the freed serfs had been given land on fair terms), the peasantry would have turned into a conservative force; and it would have opposed proletarian revolution, as it did in Western Europe, particularly in France, throughout the nineteenth century. Its conservatism might then have influenced even the urban workers, many of whom had roots in the country. A bourgeois order would have had far greater staying power than that possessed by the semi-feudal and semi-bourgeois regime. The conjunction of the two revolutions made possible the alliance of the workers and peasants for which Lenin strove; and this enabled the Bolsheviks to win the civil war and withstand foreign intervention. Although the aspirations of the workers were in implicit conflict with those of the peasants, neither of the two classes was as yet aware of this. The workers rejoiced in the *muzhiks'* triumph over the landlords; and they saw no contradiction between

C

their own striving for a collectivist economy and the peasantry's economic individualism. The contradiction became apparent and acute only towards the end of the civil war, when the peasantry, no longer inhibited by fear of the landlords' return, forcefully asserted that individualism.[1]

Henceforth the conflict between town and country and the clash between the two revolutions dominated the domestic scene of the U.S.S.R. for at least two decades, throughout the 1920s and the 1930s; and the consequences overshadow the whole of Soviet history. The vicissitudes of the drama are familiar enough. Lenin, in his last years, attempted to resolve the dilemma peacefully, by means of the New Economic Policy and a mixed economy; but by 1927 or 1928 the attempt had failed. Stalin then sought to resolve the conflict forcibly and embarked on the so-called wholesale collectivization of farming. He divorced the socialist revolution from the bourgeois one by annihilating the latter.

Karl Marx and his disciples had hoped that proletarian revolution would be free of the feverish convulsions, the false consciousness, and the fits of irrationality that had characterized the course of bourgeois revolution. They had, of course, in mind socialist revolution in its 'pure form'; and they assumed that it would take place in advanced industrial countries, on a high level of society's economic and cultural development. It is all too easy—but it is also irrelevant—to contrast these confident hopes with the welter of irrationality in this half-century of Soviet history. Much of the irrationality has originated in the contradictions between Russia's two revolutions, for these produced a long series of crises which could not be managed by normal methods of statecraft, political accommodation, or manoeuvre.

---

[1] This was the prevailing attitude, even though the peasantry itself was divided between rich and poor, and small groups of enlightened peasants formed, of their own accord, co-operatives and communes soon after the revolution and in the early 1920s.

The combination of the two revolutions became the source of Soviet weakness.

The irrationality of the Puritan and Jacobin revolutions arose largely out of the clash between the high hopes of the insurgent peoples and the bourgeois limitations of those revolutions. To the insurgent masses no revolution is ever bourgeois. They fight for freedom and equality or for the brotherhood of men and the Commonwealth. The crisis comes when the possessing classes grow impatient to have the full benefit of the gains the revolution has brought them and to accumulate wealth. As the revolution constricts them in this they contract out of it, or seek to bring it to a halt, just when the plebeian masses, desperate from privation or hunger, press for more radical social changes. This was what happened in France, at the decline of Jacobinism, when the *nouveaux riches* clamoured for the abolition of the *maximum* and for free trade. The plebeians then discovered that their revolutionary conquests were shams, that *Liberté* was merely the labourer's liberty to sell his labour force, and that *Egalité* meant that he could bargain with his employer at the labour market on nominally equal terms. In England that was the moment when the Diggers and the Levellers discovered the power of property in the Commonwealth. Cruel disillusionment sets in. Cleavages appear in the party of the revolution. The leaders are torn by conflicting loyalties. And the intensity of passion and action, which was the revolution's creative force during its ascendancy, turns into a destructive force in the period of stagnation and decline. We find much of this also in Russia early enough, immediately after the civil war, when the peasantry forced Lenin's government to proclaim respect for private property and reintroduce free trade, while the Workers' Opposition denounced this as a betrayal of socialism and clamoured for equality.

The predicament of the Russian revolution became even graver because Russia was also caught up in the contradictions

inherent in any socialist revolution occurring in an underdeveloped country. Marx speaks of the embryo of socialism that
grows and matures within the womb of bourgeois society. In
Russia, it may be said, the socialist revolution intervened at a
very early stage of the pregnancy, long before the embryo had
had the time to mature. The outcome was not a stillbirth; but
neither was it the viable body of socialism.

You may wonder what exactly do Marxists mean by this meta-
phor? The question is certainly relevant to our theme and—incidentally—to the problems of Western society as well. Marx describes how modern industry, having replaced the independent
craftsmen, artisans, and farmers by hired workers, has changed
thereby the whole process by which man sustains his life, the
process of production, transforming it from a mass of disjointed
individual pursuits into the collective and aggregate activity of
great numbers of associated producers. With division of labour
and technological advance our productive forces grow increasingly interdependent; and they become, or tend to become, socially integrated on the national or even on the international
scale. This precisely is the 'socialization' of the productive process—the embryo of socialism within the womb of capitalism.
This type of productive process calls for social control and planning; private ownership or control is at odds with it. Private
control, even as exercised by the big modern corporations, sec-
tionalizes and disorganizes an essentially integrated social mechanism, which needs to be actually and rationally integrated.

The Marxist case against capitalism rests largely, though not
exclusively, on this argument. So does its case for socialism. It
sees in the full development of the *social* character of the productive process the major historic pre-condition of socialism. Without it socialism would be a castle in the air. To try to impose
social control on a mode of production which is not inherently
social is just as incongruous and anachronistic as it is to maintain private or sectional control over the productive process that
is social.

In Russia this basic pre-condition of socialism was lacking, as it must be lacking in any underdeveloped country. Farming, in which more than three-quarters of the people earned their living, was atomized into 23 or 24 million smallholdings, controlled by the spontaneous forces of the market. Nationalized industry was a small enclave in this primitive and anarchic economy. This meant that Russia did not possess another essential prerequisite of socialism: an abundance of goods and services which society must have if it is to meet—on a high level of civilization—the needs of its members in any manner approaching equality. Not so long ago Russian industry could not even turn out the goods that any modern nation requires for its normal functioning. Yet socialism cannot be founded on want and poverty. Against these all its aspirations are powerless. Scarcity inexorably breeds inequality. Where there is not enough food, clothing, and housing for all, a minority will grasp what it can; while the rest go hungry, clothed in rags and crowded in slums. All this was bound to happen in Russia.

In addition, the real starting point was one of utter disaster. After the years of world war, civil war, and foreign intervention the little industry that Russia had possessed collapsed into ruin. Machinery and stocks were used up. Economically, the nation was thrown back by more than half a century. Townspeople burnt their furniture to warm their dwellings. Scores of millions of peasants were hit by famine and wandered over the country in search of food. The few million workers who had manned the barricades in 1917 had become dispersed and, as a coherent social force, ceased to exist. The bravest had perished in the civil war; many had taken up posts in the new administration, army, and police; great numbers had fled from the famished cities; and the few who stayed behind spent more time trading than working, became *declassés* and were swallowed up by the black markets. These were the formative circumstances at the time when the Bolsheviks, in the early 1920s, were trying to give shape to their regime and consolidate it. In doing so, they could not rely on the class of which they had considered themselves the vanguard, the class that was supposed to be the master in the new State, the mainstay of the new democracy, the chief agent of socialism. That class had physically and politically faded out. Thus, while the bourgeois revolution, despite the famine in the country, survived in the tangible realities of rural life, the socialist revolution was like a phantom suspended in a void.

These were the authentic origins of the so-called bureaucratic degeneration of the regime. In the circumstances as they were, 'proletarian dictatorship,' 'Soviet democracy,' 'workers' control of industry' were almost empty slogans, into which no one could breathe any content. The idea of Soviet democracy, as Lenin, Trotsky, and Bukharin had expounded it, presupposed the existence of an active, eternally vigilant, working class, asserting itself not only against the *ancien régime* but also against any new bureaucracy that might abuse or usurp power. As the working class was bodily not there, the Bolsheviks decided to act as its *locum tenentes* and trustees until such time as life would become more normal and a new working class would come into being. Meanwhile, they considered it their duty to exercise the 'proletarian dictatorship' on behalf of a non-existent, or almost non-existent, proletariat. That way lay bureaucratic dictatorship, uncontrolled power, and corruption by power.

It was not that the Bolsheviks were unaware of the danger. They would hardly have been startled by Lord Acton's dictum about power.[2] They would have agreed with him. Moreover, they understood something that Lord Acton and his disciples missed, namely, that property is also power, concentrated power, and that the quasi-monopolistic property of the big corporations is absolute power which acts all the more effectively when it is enfolded in a parliamentary democracy. The Bolsheviks were also quite well aware of the dangers of power in post-capitalist society—not for nothing did they dream about the withering

---

[2] 'Power tends to corrupt and absolute power corrupts absolutely.'

away of the State. I, at least, know of no book that goes deeper to the roots of corruption by power than does Lenin's (somewhat scholastically and dogmatically written) *State and Revolution*. There was thus a tragic element in Bolshevik fortunes: all their profound and acute awareness of the danger did not save them from it; and all their abhorrence of the corruption did not prevent them from succumbing to it.

They had, as a revolutionary party, no choice, unless they abdicated and divested themselves of power, yielding it in effect to their enemies whom they had just vanquished in the civil war. Saints or fools might have done this; but the Bolsheviks were neither. They found themselves unexpectedly in a position which, *mutatis mutandis*, was comparable to that of the Decembrists, Populists, and *Narodnovoltsy* in the nineteenth century, the position of a revolutionary elite, without a revolutionary class behind it. But the elite was now the government, holding a besieged fortress which it had precariously saved but which had still to be defended, rebuilt from ruins, and turned into the base of a new social order. Besieged fortresses are hardly ever ruled in a democratic manner. Victors in a civil war can rarely afford to allow freedom of expression and organization to the vanquished, especially when the latter are backed by powerful foreign states. As a rule, civil war results in the victors' monopoly of power.[3] The single-party system became for the Bolsheviks an inescapable necessity. Their own survival, and no doubt the survival of the revolution, depended on it. They had not aimed at it with any premeditation. They established it with misgivings as a temporary expedient. The single-party system went against the inclinations, the logic, and the ideas of Lenin, Trotsky, Kamenev, Bukharin, Lunacharsky, Rykov, and so many others. But then

[3] The American Civil War appears to be an exception. This, however, was a civil war which did not divide the nation as a whole or set class against class all over the United States. The North was virtually united in its determination to prevent the secession of the Southern states; its superiority and preponderance were never in danger; and there was no armed foreign intervention.

the logic of the situation took over and ran roughshod over their ideas and scruples. The temporary expedient became the norm. The single-party system acquired a permanence and a momentum of its own. By a process akin to natural selection, the party hierarchy found its leader, after Lenin's death, in Stalin, who, because of an outstanding ability allied to a despotic character and utter unscrupulousness, was best suited to wield the monopoly of power. Later we shall examine the use he made of it in transforming the social structure of the Soviet Union and see how this very transformation, which constantly kept society in a tremendous flux, helped to perpetuate his power. Yet even Stalin considered himself the trustee of the proletariat and of the revolution. Khrushchev, in his 1956 exposure of Stalin's crimes and inhumanity, said of him: 'Stalin was convinced that this was necessary for the defence of the interests of the working classes. . . . He looked at all this from the standpoint . . . of the interest of the labouring people . . . of socialism and communism. We cannot say that these were the deeds of a giddy despot. . . . In this lies the whole tragedy.' However, if the Bolsheviks at first felt entitled to act as trustees for the working class only during the interim of its dispersal and virtual absence, Stalin held autocratic power with all his might long after that, in the face of a reassembled and rapidly growing working class; and he used every device of terror and deception to prevent the workers, and the people at large, from claiming their rights and their revolutionary heritage.

The party's conscience was in perpetual conflict with these realities of the monopoly of power. As early as 1922 Lenin, pointing from his deathbed at Stalin, warned the party against the 'Big Bully,' the *dzierzhymorda*, the Great Russian chauvinist, who was coming back to oppress the weak and the helpless; and he confessed that he felt himself to be 'deeply guilty before the workers of Russia' for not having given them this warning earlier. Three years later Kamenev tried in vain to recall to a stormy Party Congress Lenin's testament. In 1926 Trotsky, at a session of the Politbureau, also pointing at Stalin, threw in his face the words: 'Gravedigger of the revolution.' 'He is the new Genghiz Khan'—this was Bukharin's terrified premonition in 1928—'he will slaughter us all . . . he is going to drown in blood the risings of the peasants.' And these were not random remarks made by a few leaders. Behind these men ever new oppositions rose, seeking to bring the party back to its revolutionary-democratic traditions and socialist commitments. This is what the Workers' Opposition and the Democratic Centralists tried to do as early as 1921 and 1922, what the Trotskyists did from 1923 onwards, the Zinovievists from 1925 till 1927, the Bukharinists in 1928 and 1929, and lesser and less articulate groups, even Stalinist ones, at various other times.

I cannot here go into the story of these struggles and purges—I have related it elsewhere. Clearly, as the successive schisms were being suppressed, the monopoly of power grew ever more narrow and rigid. At first the single party still left freedom of expression and political initiative at least to its own members. Then the ruling oligarchy deprived them of that freedom; and the monopoly of the single party became in fact a monopoly of a single faction, the Stalinist faction. In the second decade of the revolution the totalitarian monolith took shape. Finally, the rule of the single faction turned into the personal rule of its chief. The fact that Stalin could establish his autocracy only over the dead bodies of most of the original leaders of the revolution and their followers, and that he had to climb over the corpses even of good Stalinists, gives a measure of the depth and strength of the resistance he had to break.

The political metamorphoses of the regime were accompanied by a debasement of the ideas of 1917. People were taught that socialism required not merely national ownership and planning, rapid industrialization, collectivization, and popular education, but that somehow the so-called cult of the individual, crude privilege and vehement anti-egalitarianism, and omnipotence of the police were all part and parcel of the new society. Marxism, the most critical and irreverent of doctrines, was emptied of its content and reduced to a set of sophisms or quasi-ecclesiastical canons, designed to justify every one of Stalin's decrees and every one of his pseudo-theoretical whims. The devastating effects that all this had on Soviet science, art, literature, and on the country's moral climate are well known. And, as Stalinism was, over three decades, the official doctrine of a world organization, this debasement of socialism and Marxism had momentous repercussions in the international field as well, especially in the Western labour movement; and I intend to examine these in a different context.

The Russian revolution had some streaks of irrationality in common with the bourgeois revolutions of which it was the last. This is, in a sense, the bourgeois element in its character. As the master of the purges, Stalin was Cromwell's and Robespierre's descendant. His terror was far more cruel and repulsive than theirs, for he exercised power over a much longer period, in more daunting circumstances, and in a country accustomed over the ages to barbarous brutality in its rulers. Stalin, we should remember, was also the descendant of Ivan the Terrible, Peter the Great, Nicholas I, and Alexander III. Indeed, Stalinism may be described as the amalgam of Marxism with Russia's primordial and savage backwardness. In any case, in Russia the aspirations of the revolution and its realities were far wider apart than anywhere else; and so it took far more blood and far greater hypocrisy to cover up the terrible discrepancy.

In what then, it will be asked, lies the continuity of the revolution? What reality has it after all these political and ideological metamorphoses, after so many eruptions of terror and other cataclysms? Similar questions have arisen with reference to other revolutions. Where and when, for instance, did the French revolution come to a close? Was it when the Jacobins were suppressing the Commune and the *Enragés?* Or when Robespierre mounted the steps of the guillotine? At the moment of Napoleon's coronation? Or at his dethronement? Most of these events, despite their drastic character, are wrapped in ambiguity; only Napoleon's fall marks unequivocally the end of the historical cycle. In Russia a similar ambiguity surrounds events such as the Kronstadt rising of 1921, the defeat of Trotsky in 1923, his expulsion in 1927, the purges of the 1930s, Khrushchev's disclosures about Stalin in 1956, to mention only these. Sectarians will argue endlessly about these breaks in continuity and point out at which of these the revolution was 'finally' betrayed and defeated. (Curiously, Trotsky himself, in the years of his last exile, tried to persuade some of his overzealous supporters that the revolution had not come to an end with his own deportation.) These sectarian disputes have their own significance, especially for historians who may glean from them quite a few grains of truth. French historians, the best of them, are till this day divided into pro- and anti-Jacobins, Dantonists, Robespierrists, Hebertists, defenders of the Commune, Thermidorians and anti-Thermidorians, Bonapartists and anti-Bonapartists; and their controversies have always had a close bearing on the current political preoccupations of Frenchmen. I am convinced that Soviet historians will likewise be divided for many generations, just as we participants of the communist movement in the 1920s and the 1930s were, into Trotskyists, Stalinists, Bukharinists, Zinovievists, Decemists, and so on; and I hope that some of them will be able to produce, without fear or embarrassment, apologies for the Mensheviks and Social Revolutionaries as well.

But the question about the continuity of the revolution is not resolved in such disputes—it transcends them. It must be, and it is, judged by other, wider criteria. We need not go as far as Clemenceau, who once said that 'the revolution is a single block from which nothing can be detracted.' But something may be said for the Clemenceau approach, even though the 'block' is an alloy with a great deal of base metal in it.

One way of dealing with our problem is to say that the contemporaries of a revolution acknowledge its continuity by the attitudes they take up towards it, by their policies and deeds. They do so in our time as well. The great divide of 1917 still looms as large as ever in the consciousness of mankind. To our statesmen and ideologues, and even to ordinary people the issues posed by it are still unresolved. And the fact that the rulers and leaders of the Soviet Union have never stopped invoking their revolutionary origins, has also had its logic and its consequences. All of them, including Stalin, Khrushchev, and Khrushchev's successors, have had to cultivate in the minds of their people the sense of the revolution's continuity. They have had to reiterate the pledges of 1917, even while they themselves were breaking them; and they have had to restate, again and again, the Soviet Union's commitment to socialism. These pledges and commitments have been inculcated into every new generation and age group, at school and in the factory. The tradition of the revolution has dominated the Soviet system of education. This in itself is a potent factor of continuity. True enough, the pattern of the education is designed to conceal the breaks in continuity, to falsify history, and to explain away its contradictions and irrationalities. Yet, despite all this, the educational system has constantly reawakened in the mass of the people an awareness of their revolutionary heritage.

Behind these ideological and political phenomena there is the real continuity of a system based on the abolition of private ownership and the complete nationalization of industry and banking. All the changes in government, party leadership, and policies have not affected this basic and inviolable 'conquest of October.' This is the rock on which the ideological continuity rests. Property relations or forms of ownership are not a passive or indifferent factor in the development of society. We know how profoundly the change from feudal to bourgeois forms of property has altered the way of life and the shape of Western society. Now, comprehensive, full national ownership of the means of production entails an even more many-sided and fundamental long-term transformation. It would be erroneous to think that there is only a quantitative difference between the nationalization of, say, 25 per cent of industry and 100 per cent public ownership. The difference is qualitative. In a modern industrial society comprehensive public ownership is bound to create an essentially new environment for man's productive activity and cultural pursuits. Since post-revolutionary Russia was not a modern industrial society, national ownership *per se* could not create that qualitatively new environment, but only some elements of it. Even this was enough to influence decisively the evolution of the Soviet Union and give a certain unity to the processes of its social transformation.

I have spoken about the incongruity of the attempt to establish social control over a productive process which is not social in character, and also about the impossibility of a socialism founded on want and scarcity. The whole history of the Soviet Union in these fifty years has been a struggle, partly successful and partly not, to resolve this incongruity and to overcome want and scarcity. This meant, in the first instance, intensive industrialization as a means towards an end, not an end in itself. Feudal and even bourgeois property relations may be compatible with economic stagnation or a sluggish tempo of growth. National ownership is not, especially when it has been established in an underdeveloped country by way of a proletarian revolution. The system carries within it the compulsion to rapid advance, the necessity to strive for abundance, and the urge to develop that social productive process which calls for rational social control. In the course of the advance, which was made for Russia far more difficult than it need have been by wars, arms races, and bureaucratic waste, ever new contradictions arose; and means and ends were perpetually confused. As national wealth was being accumulated, the mass of consumers, who are also the producers, were exposed to continued and even aggravated want and poverty; and bureaucratic control over every aspect of national life substituted itself for social control and responsibility. The order of priorities was as it were reversed. The forms of socialism had been forged before the content, the economic and cultural substance, was available; and as the content was being produced the forms deteriorated or were distorted. At first, the socio-political institutions created by the revolution towered high above the actual level of the nation's material and cultural existence; then, as that level rose, the socio-political order was depressed beneath it by the sheer weight of bureaucracy and Stalinism. Even the end was brought down to the level of the means: the ideal image of a classless society was dragged down to the miseries of this period of transition and to the crude necessities of a primitive accumulation of wealth.

This reversal of social priorities, this confusion of ends and means, and the resulting disharmony between the forms and the content of national life are the deepest sources of the crises, the ferments, and the agitation of the post-Stalin era. Bureaucratic control, that substitute for social control, has become a brake on further progress; and the nation is longing to manage its own wealth and to be master of its own destinies. It does not quite know how to voice its aspirations and what to do about them. Decades of totalitarian rule and monolithic discipline have robbed the people of their capacity for self-expression, spontaneous action, and self-organization. The ruling groups tinker with economic reforms, loosen their grip on the nation's mind, and yet do what they can to keep the people inarticulate and passive. These are the limits of the official de-Stalinization, behind which there lurks an unofficial de-Stalinization, a widespread expectation of root-and-branch change. Both the official policy and the unofficial moods feed on undispelled or revived memories of the early heroic period of the revolution with its far greater freedom, rationality, and humanity. This apparent return to the past, with the ceaseless pilgrimage to Lenin's tomb, probably covers an awkward pause between the Stalin era and some new start in the Soviet Union's creative thinking and historic action. Whatever may be the truth, the malaise, the heart-searchings, and the gropings of the post-Stalin era testify in their own way to the continuity of the revolutionary epoch.

III

The Social Structure

Let us now examine in general terms the changes that have taken place in the social structure of the U.S.S.R.—such a survey may present something like an interim sociological balance sheet of these fifty years.

Discussing earlier the question of the revolution's continuity, I underlined the significance of the circumstance that the State, and not 'private enterprise' or the big capitalist corporation, has been in charge of the industrialization and modernization of the Soviet Union. This fact has determined the dynamics of Soviet economic growth and the character of the social transformation. There is no need to dwell here on the strictly economic aspect of the problem. We all know that the Soviet Union has risen from the position of the most backward of the great European nations to the rank of the world's second industrial power—the international consequences of its ascendancy have been with us all the time during these last decades. Still, I must confess, as one of those who witnessed at close quarters the early phases of this rise and the appalling difficulties that attended it, that I have not accustomed myself to take the outcome for granted. I would not have believed, in say 1930, and not even in 1940, that the Soviet Union would progress quite as rapidly as it did and that by 1967 it would produce—to give only one indication—100 million tons of steel per year. This is more than Great Britain, the Federal German Republic, France, and Italy produce together, and only 20 million tons less than is turned out by the steel mills of the United States. This is the foundation for an engineering industry and an output of producer goods approximately as large as the American. The consumer industries are, of course, lagging far behind. But leaving out further economic statistics, I shall rather consider here the sociological accompaniments and consequences of the economic advance.

Before we proceed any further we ought, perhaps, to remind ourselves that these fifty years have not been a single uninterrupted period of growth and development. Seven or eight of the fifty years were taken up by armed hostilities which resulted in severe setbacks and widespread destruction, unparalleled in any other belligerent country. Another twelve or thirteen years were spent on replacing the losses. The actual periods of growth cover the years from 1928 to 1941 and from 1950 onwards, about thirty years in all. And in these years an unusually high proportion of Soviet resources, about one-quarter of the national income on the average, was absorbed in the arms races that preceded and followed the Second World War. If one could calculate the advance in ideal units of truly peaceful years, one would conclude that the Soviet Union achieved its progress within twenty or, at the most, twenty-five years. This has to be kept in mind when one tries to assess the performance. But, of course, present Soviet society is the product of the turmoil of this half-century so that in its development gain and loss, construction and destruction, have been inseparable; and the combination of productive effort, unproductive work, and waste has affected both the material life and the spiritual climate of the U.S.S.R.

The first and most striking feature of the transformed scene is the massive urbanization of the U.S.S.R. Since the revolution the town population has grown by over 100 million people. Here again a corrective in the time scale is needed. The first decade after 1917 was marked by a depopulation of the cities and a slow reverse movement. The effect of the Second World War was the same, at least in European Russia. The periods of intensive urbanization were between the years 1930 and 1940 and between 1950 and 1965. About 800 big and medium-sized towns and over 2000 small urban settlements were built. In 1926 there were only 26 million town dwellers. In 1966 their number was about 125 million. In the last fifteen years alone the urban population has increased by 53 or 54 million people, that is by as much as the entire population of the British Isles. Within the lifetime of a generation the percentage of the town dwellers in the total population has risen from 15 to about 55 per cent; and it is fast climbing up to 60 per cent. In the United States—to take the previous record in this field—it took over 160 years for the urban population to increase by 100 million people; or, if the more relevant percentual comparison is made, it took a full century, from 1850 to 1950, for the proportion of the town dwellers to rise from 15 to 60 per cent. Throughout those hundred years the phenomenal growth of the American cities and towns was stimulated and facilitated by mass immigration, influx of foreign capital and skill, and immunity from foreign invasion and wartime destruction, not to speak of the inducements of climate. Soviet urbanization, in tempo and scale, is without parallel in history. Such a change in social structure, even if it had taken place in more favourable circumstances, would have created huge and baffling problems in housing, settlement, health, and education; and Soviet circumstances were as if designed to intensify and magnify beyond measure the turmoil and the shocks.

Only a small proportion of the expansion was due to natural growth or to the migration of townspeople. The mass of the new town dwellers were peasants, shifted from the villages, year after year, and directed to industrial labour. Like the old advanced nations of the West, the Soviet Union found the main reserve of industrial manpower in the peasantry. In the early stages the growth of capitalist enterprise in the West was often accompanied by the forcible expropriation of farmers—in Britain by the 'enclosures'—and by draconic labour legislation. Later the West relied in the main on the spontaneous work of the labour market, with its laws of supply and demand, to bring the required manpower to industry. This euphemism means that in the course of many decades, if not of centuries, rural overpopulation, and sometimes famine, threw great masses of redundant hands onto the labour market. In the Soviet Union the State secured the supply of labour by means of planning and direction. Its dominant economic position was the decisive factor; without it, it would hardly have been possible to carry out so gigantic a transformation within so short a time.

The transfer of the rural population began in earnest in the early 1930s, and it was closely connected with the collectivization of farming, which enabled the government's agencies to lay hands on the surplus of manpower on the farms and to move it to industry. The beginnings of the process were extremely difficult and involved the use of much force and violence. The habits of settled industrial life, regulated by the factory siren, which had in other countries been inculcated into the workers, from generation to generation, by economic necessity and legislation, were lacking in Russia. The peasants had been accustomed to work in their fields according to the rhythm of Russia's severe nature, to toil from sunrise to sunset in the summer and to drowse on the tops of their stoves most of the winter. They had now to be forced and conditioned into an entirely new routine of work. They resisted, worked sluggishly, broke or damaged tools, and shifted restlessly from factory to factory and from mine to mine. The government imposed discipline by means of harsh labour codes, threats of deportation, and actual deportation to forced labour camps. Lack of housing and acute shortages of consumer goods, due in large measure to deliberate acts of an anti-consumptionist policy—the government was bent on obtaining the maximum output of producer goods and munitions—aggravated the hardships and the turbulence. It was common in the cities, even quite recently, for several families to share a single room and a kitchen; and in the industrial settlements, masses of workers were herded in barracks for many years. Crime was rampant. At the same time, however, many millions of men and women received primary or even secondary education, were trained in industrial skills, and settled down to the new way of life.

As time went on, social friction and conflicts engendered by the upheaval lessened. Since the Second World War the feats of Soviet industry and arms have appeared to justify retrospectively even the violence, the suffering, the blood, and the tears. But it may be held, as I have held through all these decades, that without the violence, the blood, and the tears, the great work of construction might have been done far more efficiently and with healthier social, political, and moral after-effects. Whatever the truth of the matter, the transformation of the social structure continues; and continues without such forcible stimulation. Year after year the urban population is expanding on the same scale as before; and the process, though planned and regulated, obeys its own rhythm. In the 1930s the government had to drag a sullen mass of peasants into the towns; in this last decade or so it has been confronted by a spontaneous rush of people from the country to towns; and it has had to exert itself and make rural life a little more attractive in order to keep young labour on the farms. But the present population trend will probably continue; and in another ten or fifteen years, three-quarters of the population may well live in towns.

The industrial workers, the small minority of 1917, now form the largest social class. The State employs about 78 million people in workshops and offices—it employed 27 million after the end of the Second World War. Well over 50 million people work in primary and manufacturing industries, in building, transport, communications, and on State-owned farms. The rest earn their livelihood in various services—13 million of them in health, education, and scientific research. It is not easy to distinguish

with any precision the numbers of manual workers and technicians from those of office workers, because Soviet statistics lump
them together—the sociological significance of this will be discussed later. The number of the workers proper may be put at
between 50 and 55 million.

The working class is highly stratified. Stalin's labour policy
centred on differential scales of salaries and wages and raised the
labour aristocracy high above the mass of the underpaid semi-
skilled and unskilled, workers. To some extent this was justified
by the need to offer incentives to skill and efficiency; but the
discrepancies in wages went far beyond. Their actual extent was
and still is surrounded by extraordinary secrecy. Since the 1930s
the government has not published the relevant data about the
national wage structure, and students have had to content
themselves with fragmentary information. Throughout the Stalin era a ferocious witch-hunt against the levellers—or the 'petty
bourgeois egalitarians'—was in progress; but it was less effective
than it appeared to be, and certainly less so than the political
witch-hunts.

The suppression of data about the structure of wages and
salaries indicates with what guilty conscience the ruling groups,
under Stalin and after him, have pursued their anti-egalitarian
policy. No such guilty conscience prevents our captains of industry from advertising their profits or inhibits our governments
from revealing the facts about our scales of wages and salaries.
Of course, nothing like our 'normal' inequality between earned
and unearned incomes exists in the Soviet Union. The inequality is in the earned incomes. Yet to expose its full extent would
evidently be too risky and dangerous an undertaking for any Soviet government. The discrepancies in workers' earnings seem
similar to those that can be found in most other countries; and
they are narrowed by the greater value of the Soviet Union's
more comprehensive social services. In recent years the wage
structure has been overhauled again and again. The first period
of de-Stalinization brought an evident reduction of inequalities

the extent of which it is difficult to assess. Subsequently the new wage policy has met with increasing resistance on the part of the managers and the labour aristocracy. In a continuously and rapidly expanding economy, however, high social mobility does not allow the stratification to become unduly rigid. Great masses of workers are constantly trained for skilled jobs and pass from lower to higher income groups.

The social and cultural stratification of the working class is sometimes even more important than the economic one. This is a subject which does not lend itself to a clear-cut sociological description or analysis; all I can do here is to try to convey a general idea of it and to indicate its complexity. The prodigious growth of the working class has resulted in many social and cultural discrepancies and incongruities, reflecting the successive phases of industrialization and their overlapping. Each phase brought into being a different layer of the working class and produced significant cleavages. The bulk of the working class is strongly marked by its peasant origins. There are only very few working-class families who have been settled in town since before the revolution and have any sort of industrial tradition and memories of pre-revolutionary class struggle. In effect, the oldest layer of workers is the one which formed itself during the reconstruction period of the 1920s. Its adaptation to the rhythm of industrial life was relatively easy—these workers came to the factory of their own accord and were not yet subjected to strict regimentation. Their children are the most settled and the most distinctly urban element of the industrial population. From their ranks came the *vydvizhentsy*, the managerial elements and the labour aristocracy of the 1930s and 1940s. Those who remained in the ranks were the last Soviet workers to engage freely, under the New Economic Policy, in trade union activities, even in strikes, and to enjoy a certain freedom of political expression.

The contrast between this and the next layer is extremely sharp. Twenty-odd million peasants were shifted to the towns during the 1930s. Their adaptation was painful and jerky. For a long time they remained uprooted villagers, town dwellers against their will, desperate, anarchic, and helpless. They were broken to the habits of factory work and kept under control by ruthless drill and discipline. It was they who gave the Soviet towns the grey, miserable, semi-barbarous look that so often astonished foreign visitors. They brought into industry the *muzhiks*' crude individualism. Official policy played on it, prodding the industrial recruits to compete with one another for bonuses, premiums, and multiple piece rates. Worker was thus turned against worker at the factory bench; and pretexts of 'socialist competition' were used to prevent the formation and manifestation of any class solidarity. The terror of the 1930s left an indelible imprint on the men of this category. Most of them, now in their fifties, are probably—through no fault of theirs—the most backward element among Soviet workers—uneducated, acquisitive, servile. Only in its second generation could this layer of the working class live down the initial shocks of urbanization.

The peasants who came to the factories in the aftermath of the Second World War still experienced the trying living conditions, virtual homelessness, severe labour discipline, and the terror. But most had come to town voluntarily, eager to escape from devastated and famished villages. They had been prepared for industrial discipline by years of army life and found in their new places an environment better able to absorb and assimilate newcomers than were the towns and factory settlements of the 1930s. The process of adaptation was less painful. It became easier still for the next batches of trainees who arrived in the factories during the post-Stalin years, when the old labour codes were abolished, and who settled down to their occupations in relative freedom from want and fear. The youngest age groups, the latest immigrants, and the town-bred children of the earlier ones have arrived in the workshops with a self-confidence which was altogether lacking in their elders and have played a big part in reforming outdated labour routines and in changing the climate of Soviet factory life. Nearly all of them have ('complete or incomplete') secondary education, and many take extra-mural academic courses. They have often clashed with their less efficient and less civilized foremen and managers. This is probably the most progressive group of the Soviet working class, comprising the builders of nuclear plants, computers, and space ships, workers as productive as their American counterparts, even though the average Soviet productivity per man-hour is still only 40 per cent of American productivity or even less. The low average is, of course, due to the great diversity of Soviet industrial manpower, to the many different and uneven levels of culture and efficiency, which I have just tried to trace. Even so, the average Soviet productivity is somewhat ahead of the West European; and it is worth recalling that in the 1920s, when American productivity was about one-third of what it is at present, Soviet production per man-hour was only one-tenth of the American.

This all too sketchy description gives us only a general idea of the extraordinary social and cultural heterogeneity of the Soviet working class. The process of transplantation and expansion was too rapid and stormy to allow for the mutual assimilation of the diverse layers, the formation of a common outlook, and the growth of class solidarity. We have seen how a few years after the revolution the shrinkage and disintegration of the working class had permitted the bureaucracy to establish itself as the dominant social force. What came after that allowed it to consolidate this position. The manner in which the new factory hands were recruited and the furious pace of growth kept the working class in a state of permanent disarray and fragmentation, unable to gain cohesion, balance, unity, and to find a sociopolitical identity. The workers were incapacitated by the very swelling of their numbers. The bureaucracy did what it could to keep them in this state. Not only did it play them against one another at the factory bench; it fanned all their mutual dislikes and antagonisms. It denied them the right to raise demands and to defend themselves through the trade unions. But these devices and the terror would not have been as effective as they were, if the working class had not been torn by its own centrifugal forces. What made matters worse was that the constant promotion of bright and energetic workers to managerial posts deprived the rank and file of potential mouthpieces and leaders. While education was scarce among the toilers, this brain drain had important consequences: the social mobility which benefited some of the workers, condemned the rest to social and political debility.

If this analysis is correct then the prospect for the future may be more hopeful. An objective process of consolidation and integration is taking place in the working class, and it is accompanied by a growth of social awareness. This—as well as the requirements of technological progress—has compelled the ruling group to sweep away the old factory discipline and to concede to the workers much more elbow room than they had in the Stalin era. There is still a long way from this to freedom of expression and to workers' genuine participation in control over industry. Yet as the working class grows more educated, homogeneous, and self-confident, its aspirations are likely to focus on these demands. And if this happens the workers may re-enter the political stage as an independent factor, ready to challenge the bureaucracy, and ready to resume the struggle for emancipation in which they scored so stupendous a victory in 1917, but which for so long they have not been able to follow up.

The obverse side of the expansion of the working class is the shrinkage of the peasantry. Forty years ago rural smallholders made up more than three-quarters of the nation; at present the collectivized farmers constitute only one-quarter. How desperately the peasants resisted this trend, what furious violence was let loose against them, how they were forced to contribute to the sinews of industrialization, and how resentfully and sluggishly they have tilled the land under the collectivist dispensation—all this is now common knowledge. But, as Professor But-

terfield says in a somewhat different context: 'It is the tendency
of contemporaries to estimate the revolution too exclusively by
its atrocities, while posterity always seems to err through its inability to take these into account or vividly appreciate them.'[1]
As one who witnessed the collectivization in the early 1930s and
severely criticized its forcible methods, I would like to reflect
here on the tragic fate of the Russian peasantry. Under the *ancien régime* the Russian countryside was periodically swept by
famine, as China's countryside was and as India's still is. In the
intervals between the famines, uncounted (statistically unno-
ticed) millions of peasants and peasant children died of malnutrition and disease, as they still do in so many underdeveloped
countries.[2] The old system was hardly less cruel towards the
peasantry than Stalin's government, only its cruelty appeared to
be part of the natural order of things, which even the moralist's
sensitive conscience is inclined to take for granted. This cannot
excuse or mitigate the crimes of Stalinist policy; but it may put
the problem into proper perspective. Those who argue that all
would have been well if only the *muzhiks* had been left alone,
the idealizers of the old rural way of life and of the peasantry's
individualism, are purveying an idyll which is a figment of their
imagination. The old primitive smallholding was, in any case,
too archaic to survive into the epoch of industrialization. It has
not survived either in this country or in the United States; and

[1] H. Butterfield, *Christianity and History* (London, 1949), p. 143.
[2] This is, for instance, what *The Times* correspondent in Delhi wrote on
3 February 1967 under the title 'Bihar villagers now slowly starving'; 'Re-
ports from the districts worst affected suggest that slow starvation has marked
the poorest of the village communities already.' In effect 'perhaps 20 million
landless labourers in the afflicted areas of Eastern Uttar Pradesh as well as
Bihar' are threatened by famine, unless they are fed by the administration
until the autumn. The horror was aggravated by a simultaneous threat of
water famine: '. . . once the village wells dry up, the people will set off in
search of water. Large numbers of people on the move in search of water
must greatly complicate the task of giving them food.' Simultaneously, *Le
Monde* reported that 50 per cent of the children of Senegal were dying before the age of five because of malnutrition and disease. These facts were re
ported, as small news items, on one day only.

even in France, its classical homeland, we have witnessed a dramatic shrinkage of the peasantry in recent years. In Russia the smallholding was a formidable obstacle to the nation's progress: it was unable to provide food for the growing urban population; it could not even feed the children of the overpopulated countryside. The only reasonable alternative to forcible collectivization lay in some form of collectivization or co-operation based on the consent of the peasantry. Just how realistic this alternative was for the U.S.S.R. no one can now say with any certainty. What is certain is that forcible collectivization has left a legacy of agricultural inefficiency and antagonism between town and country which the Soviet Union has not yet lived down.

These calamities have been aggravated by yet another blow the peasantry has suffered, a blow surpassing all the atrocities of the collectivization. Most of the 20 million men that the Soviet Union lost on the battlefields of the Second World War were peasants. So huge was the gap in rural manpower that during the late 1940s and in the 1950s in most villages only women, children, cripples, and old men were seen working in the fields. This accounted in some measure for the stagnant condition of farming, and for much else besides: for dreadful strains on family relations, sexual life, and rural education; and for more than the normal amount of apathy and inertia in the countryside.

The peasantry's weight in the nation's social and political life has, in consequence of all these events, steeply declined. The condition of farming remains a matter of grave concern, for it affects the standard of living and the morale of the urban population. A poor harvest is still a critical event, politically; and a succession of bad harvests contributed to Khrushchev's downfall in 1964. Nor has the peasantry been truly integrated into the new industrial structure of society. Much of the old individualistic farming, of the pettiest and most archaic kind, is still going on behind the façade of the *kolkhoz*. Within a stone's throw of automated computer-run concerns there are still shabby and Oriental bazaars crowded with rural traders. Yet the time when the Bolsheviks were afraid that the peasantry might be the agent of a capitalist restoration has long passed. True, there are rich *kolkhozes* and poor ones; and here and there a crafty *muzhik* manages to by-pass all rules and regulations and to rent land, employ hired labour surreptitiously, and make a lot of money. However, these survivals of primitive capitalism are hardly more than a marginal phenomenon. If the present population trend— the migration from country to town—continues, the peasantry will go on shrinking; and there will probably be a massive shift from the collectively owned to the State-owned farms. Eventually, farming may be expected to be 'Americanized' and to employ only a small fraction of the nation's manpower.

Meanwhile, even though the peasantry is dwindling, the *muzhik* tradition still looms very large in Russian life, in custom and manners, in language, literature, and the arts. Although a majority of Russians are already living in town, most Russian novels, perhaps four out of five, still take village-life as their theme and the *muzhik* as their chief character. Even in his exit he casts a long melancholy shadow on the new Russia.

And now we come to what is in any sociological description of the U.S.S.R. the most complex and puzzling problem, that of the bureaucracy, the managerial groups, the specialists, and the intelligentsia. Their numbers and specific weight have grown enormously. Between 11 and 12 million specialists and administrators are employed in the national economy, compared with only half a million in the 1920s, and fewer than 200,000 before the revolution. To these we must add between two and three million regular members of the political hierarchies and of the military establishment. In sheer numbers all these groups, amounting to about one-fifth of the total of those employed by the State, are almost as large as the collectivized peasantry (the *kolkhozes* have only 17 million members). Their social weight is, of course, immeasurably greater. We must not, however, lump all these groups together and label them as the bureaucracy or the managerial class. A sharp distinction ought to be made between the specialists and administrators with higher education and those with only a secondary one. The actual managerial elements are in the former category, although they are not identical with it. The specialists with higher education form about 40 per cent of the total, i.e. over 4.5 million people, or perhaps 5.5 if party cadres and military personnel are included.

Is this then the privileged bureaucracy at which Trotsky once pointed as the new enemy of the workers? Or is this Djilas's New Class? (Trotsky, as you may remember, did not take the view that the bureaucracy was a new class.) I must admit that I hesitate to answer these questions too categorically. I cannot here go into the semantics of the problem and discuss the definition of class. Let me say only this: I make a distinction between economic or social inequality and class antagonism. The difference between highly paid skilled workers and unskilled labourers is an example of an inequality which does not amount to class antagonism; it is a difference within the same social class. To my mind Djilas's view of the 'new class of exploiters' and similar ideas about the Soviet 'managerial society' are simplifications which, far from clarifying the issue, obscure it. The status of the privileged groups in Soviet society is more ambiguous than the one or the other label suggests. They are a hybrid element; they are and they are not a class. They have certain features in common with the exploiting classes of other societies; and they lack some of the latter's essential characteristics. They enjoy material and other advantages which they defend stubbornly and brutally. Here again we should beware of sweeping generalizations. About one-third of the total number of specialists are poorly paid teachers—the Soviet press has recently voiced many complaints about their living conditions. The same is true about most of half a million doctors. Many of the two million engineers, agronomists, and statisticians earn less than the wage of a highly skilled worker. Their standard of living is comparable to that of our lower middle class. This is admittedly well above the standard of living of the unskilled and semi-skilled workers. But it would be poor sociology, Marxist or otherwise, to condemn this modest prosperity as based on the exploitation of labour. Only the upper strata of the bureaucracy, of the party hierarchy, the managerial groups and the military personnel, live in conditions comparable to those enjoyed by the rich and the *nouveaux riches* in capitalist society. It is impossible to define the size of these groups—let me repeat that statistical data about their numbers and their incomes are carefully concealed. What these groups have in common with any exploiting class—I am using the term in the Marxist sense—is that their incomes are at least partly derived from the 'surplus value' produced by the workers. Moreover, they dominate Soviet society economically, politically, and culturally.

But what this so-called new class lacks is property. They own neither means of production nor land. Their material privileges are confined to the sphere of consumption. Unlike the managerial elements in our society, they are not able to turn any part of their income into capital: they cannot save, invest, and accumulate wealth in the durable and expansive form of industrial stock or of large financial assets. They cannot bequeath wealth to their descendants; they cannot, that is, perpetuate themselves as a class.[3] Trotsky once predicted that the Soviet bureaucracy would fight for the right to bequeath their possessions to their children and that they might seek to expropriate the State and become the shareholding owners of trusts and concerns. This prediction, made over thirty years ago, has not come true so far. The Maoists say that capitalism is already being re-

---

[3] They can, however, deposit money with savings banks at a very low interest rate. In 1963 nearly 14 million people had savings accounts; and the average deposit was 260 roubles. The average conceals discrepancies between amounts of money deposited by various individuals. But as few people are likely to put into a bank savings smaller than 260 roubles, the discrepancies are not likely to be socially important. In the U.S.S.R. people with high incomes prefer to spend on durable consumer goods such as cars and *dachas* rather than keep accounts in government-controlled banks.

stored in the Soviet Union; presumably they refer to the present decentralization of State control over industry. The evidence for these assertions has been less than scanty so far. Theoretically, it is possible that the present reaction against the Stalinist over-centralized economic control may stimulate neo-capitalist tend-encies among industrial managers. I think that signs of some such development may be detected in Yugoslavia—I would not put it higher than that. Yet it is unlikely that such tendencies should gain the upper hand in the U.S.S.R., if only because the abandonment of central economic planning would be a crip-pling blow to Russia's national interest and position in the world.

Speculation apart, the fact that the Soviet bureaucracy has not so far obtained for itself ownership in the means of production accounts for a certain precariousness and perishableness of its social domination. Property has always been the foundation of any class supremacy. The cohesion and unity of any class de-pends on it. Property is for the class that owns it a character-forming factor. It is also the positive element to the defence of which the class rallies. The battle cry of any possessing class is the 'sanctity of property,' and not just the right to exploit others. The privileged groups of Soviet society are not united by any comparable ties. They are in command of industry, as our busi-ness managers are; and they exercise command in an absolute manner. But behind our business managers there are the share-holders, especially the big ones. Soviet managers have not only to acknowledge that all shares belong to the nation, but to pro-fess that they act on the nation's behalf, and especially on behalf of the working class. Whether they are able to keep up this pre-tence or not depends solely on political circumstances. The work-ers may allow them to keep it up or they may not. They may, like a sluggish lot of shareholders, accept bad managers; or they may dismiss them. In other words, bureaucratic domination rests on nothing more stable than a state of political equilibrium. This is—in the long run—a far more fragile foundation for social dominance than is any established structure of property relations sanctified by law, religion, and tradition. There has been much talk recently about the antagonism, in the Soviet Union and Eastern Europe, between the political hierarchies and the technocrats; and some young theorists treat these two groups as fully fledged and opposed social classes, and speak about their 'class struggle' very much as we used to speak about the struggle between landlords and capitalists. The technocrats, one is told, with whom the workers may ally themselves, aim at overthrowing the 'central political hierarchy' which has usurped power since the revolution. Yet if the 'new class' that has ruled the Soviet Union all these decades has consisted solely of the 'central political hierarchy,' then its identity is very elusive indeed. Its composition has been repeatedly and sweepingly changed in purge after purge, during Stalin's lifetime and after. Indeed, this 'new class' looks very much like a sociologist's Cheshire cat.

In truth, Soviet bureaucracy has exercised power greater than that wielded by any possessing class in modern times; and yet its position is weaker and more vulnerable than that normally held by any such class. Its power is exceptional because it is economic, political, and cultural at the same time. Yet, paradoxically, each of these elements of power has had its origin in an act of liberation. The bureaucracy's economic prerogatives are derived from the abolition of private property in industry and finance; the political ones from the workers' and peasants' total victory over the *ancien régime*; and the cultural ones from the assumption by the State of full responsibility for the people's education and cultural development. Because of the workers' inability to maintain the supremacy they held in 1917, each of these acts of liberation turned into its opposite. The bureaucracy became the master of a masterless economy; and it established a political and cultural tutelage over the nation. But the conflict between the origins of the power and its character, between the liberating uses for which it was intended and the uses to which it has been put, has perpetually generated high political tensions and recurrent

E

purges, which have again and again demonstrated the lack of social cohesion in the bureaucracy. The privileged groups have not solidified into a new class. They have not eradicated from the popular mind the acts of liberation from which they derive their power; nor have they been able to convince the masses—or even themselves—that they have used the power in a manner compatible with those acts. In other words, the 'new class' has not obtained for itself the sanction of social legitimacy. It must constantly conceal its own identity, which the bourgeoisie and the landlords have never had to do. It has the sense of being history's bastard.

I have already mentioned the guilty conscience that compels the ruling groups to lump together 'workers' and 'employees' in one statistical total and to make a State secret of the wage structure and of the distribution of the national income. The 'new class' thus disappears in the huge grey mass of 'workers and employees.' It hides its face and conceals its share in the national cake. After so many witch-hunts against the levellers it dare not affront the egalitarianism of the masses. As one Western observer neatly put it: 'Whereas in our middle classes the rule is to keep *up* with the Joneses, in the Soviet Union the privileged people must always remember to keep *down* with the Joneses.' This brings home to us something of the ethos of Soviet society, something of its underlying morality, and, again, something of the vitality and compelling force of the revolutionary tradition.

Moreover, the Soviet Joneses are coming up *en masse*. They are being educated *en masse*. Where social stratification is based solely on income and function, and not on property, the progress of mass education is a powerful and ultimately irresistible force for equality. We have seen that the number of Soviet specialists with higher and secondary education has risen, within a relatively short period, from half a million to 12 million. This goes on. In a society expanding on so vast a scale and so rapidly, the privileged groups have to be constantly absorbing new plebeian and proletarian elements, whom they find increasingly difficult to assimilate, which again prevents the 'new class' from consolidating itself socially and politically.[4]

I have referred to the brain drain which, over a long period, reduced the Soviet working class to a meek and inert mass. Now an opposite process is taking place: mass education is spreading faster than the privileged groups expand, faster even than the needs of industrialization require. It is indeed running ahead of the country's economic resources. According to recent educational surveys, 80 per cent of the pupils of Soviet secondary schools, mostly children of workers, demand to be admitted to the universities. The universities cannot accept them. The expansion of higher education cannot keep pace with the spread of secondary education; and industry needs hands. And so these huge numbers of young people are being turned away from the gates of the universities towards the factories. For all the difficulties that this situation creates, it is also unique. It illustrates with dramatic effect how the gulf between brain and brawn is in fact narrowing in the U.S.S.R. The immediate consequence is a relative overproduction of the intelligentsia which is being pressed into the ranks of the working class. The worker-intellectuals are a creative but potentially also an explosive element in the body politic. The force of the revolutionary tradition has been great enough to compel the bureaucracy to give the workers much more education than has been required on narrow economic grounds, and perhaps more than is safe for the privileged groups. It may be argued that the bureaucracy is thus breeding

[4] In 1966, 68 million pupils received instruction in schools of all grades, compared with 10 or 11 million before the revolution. For demographic reasons (the low birth rate of the war years) the number of pupils was, at 46–48 million, stationary in the two decades of the 1940s and 1950s. In the last seven years, however, it has grown by 22 million. 47 millions were at primary and secondary schools; 3.6 millions at the universities; 3.3 millions at technical colleges; 13 million received instruction at adult educational classes, among them about 2 million workers and technicians who took university courses without interrupting their normal work. Since 1950 the number of university students has trebled.

its own grave-diggers. Such a view may well overdramatize the prospect. But clearly the dynamics of Soviet society are becoming enriched with new contradictions and tensions which will not, I think, allow it to stagnate and ossify under the domination of a 'new class.'

IV

Stalemate in Class Struggle

We have surveyed the Soviet scene so far only from the domestic angle, without referring to international events and pressures. But, of course, the internal evolution of the Soviet Union cannot be isolated from its world context, from the international balance of forces and great power diplomacy, or from the state of the labour movement in the West and the colonial revolutions in the East. All these factors have had an almost continuous impact on internal Soviet developments and all, in their turn, have been affected by the latter.

'The October revolution,' Lenin used to say, 'has broken, in Russia, the weakest link in the chain of international imperialism.' This suggestive image epitomizes the thinking of early Bolshevism about itself and the world. The October revolution is not considered here a purely Russian phenomenon: what happened in the 'weakest link of the chain' was obviously not a self-sufficient act. Despite the Russian break-through, imperialism—the expansive capitalism of the big industrial-financial corporations—remained the dominant force in the world's economy and politics; the working classes had still to break various other links of the chain. Where, how, and how soon would they do it? —these were the questions. Would one or several strong links give way in the West? Or would it be another weak link in the East, in China or India? Whatever the answer, the underlying conception was one of the revolution's universality and of the international character, scope, and destiny of socialism.

This idea was deeply rooted in classical Marxism; and it was not just an ideological postulate but a conclusion drawn from a comprehensive analysis of bourgeois society. Of course, even in 1789 men like Condorcet and Cloots and the cosmopolitans among the Jacobins dreamt about the universal Republic of the Peoples. But their dream was at odds with the real possibilities and tasks of their time. All their revolution could do was to take France out of the age of the feudal and post-feudal divisions into that of the modern nation-state. It could not go beyond the nation-state. The material conditions for any supra-national organization of society did not exist. Only in the nineteenth century did industrial capitalism *begin* to produce them. With its mechanical technology and international division of labour it created the world market, and with it the economic potentiality of a world society. As early as 1847 Marx and Engels wrote in the *Communist Manifesto:*

> Modern industry has established the world market . . . has given an immense development to commerce, navigation, and communication by land. . . . The need of a constantly expanding market for its products chases the bourgeoisie over the whole surface of the globe. . . . The bourgeoisie has given . . . a cosmopolitan character to production and consumption in every country. To the great chagrin of the reactionaries, the bourgeoisie has drawn from under the feet of industry the national ground on which it stood. . . . In place of the old local and national seclusion and self-sufficiency, we now have the many-sided intercourse of nations and their universal interdependence.

Socialism had to begin where capitalism ended. Basing itself on the facts of the 'many-sided intercourse and interdependence of nations' it would organize their productive forces on an international scale and enable society to recast its way of life accordingly. In capitalism the urge towards international integration works haphazardly, blindly, by fits and starts, as one of many contradictory trends; under imperialism it finds a distorted expression in the conquest and economic domination of the weak nations by the strong. Socialism, seizing the possibility which capitalism had opened up but not realized, would consciously create the international society. To Marx, Engels, and their close friends these were elementary ideas, almost truisms, on which they did not need to waste words. More than forty years after the *Communist Manifesto*, in 1890, Engels wrote in a message to French socialists:

> It was your great countryman Saint-Simon who first saw that the alliance of the three great Western nations— France, England, Germany—is the primary international condition of the political and social emancipation of the whole of Europe. I hope to see this alliance, the nucleus of the European alliance which will once and for all put an end to the wars of Cabinets and races, realized by the proletarians of these three nations.

What a reflection it is on the slowness of our official minds that it took three-quarters of a century—indeed the hundred and twenty years since the *Communist Manifesto*—before our statesmen and opinion makers got just an inkling of some such idea and presented a timid conservative version—or should one say a travesty?—of it in the so-called Common Market.

How consistently classical Marxism repudiated any pretension of national self-sufficiency in socialism may be seen from the following words which Engels, shortly before his death, addressed to Paul Lafargue, the famous French socialist. Engels warned Lafargue against an inclination to exalt French socialism unduly and attribute to it a superior or exceptional role.

But neither the French [he wrote] nor the Germans, nor
the English, will have all to themselves the glory of having
crushed capitalism. France . . . may *perhaps* give the
signal [for the revolution], but it will be in Germany . . .
that the issue will be decided; and even France and Germany will not secure definite victory as long as England
remains in the hands of the bourgeoisie. The emancipation of the proletariat can be only an international event;
you render it impossible if you try to make it simply a
French event. Exclusive French leadership of the bourgeois revolution—though it was inevitable because of the
stupidity and cowardice of other nations—led—you know
where?—to Napoleon, to conquest, and to invasion by the
Holy Alliance. To wish to attribute to France the same
role in the future is to pervert the international proletarian
movement and even . . . to render France ridiculous, for
people outside your frontiers mock at these pretensions.

I have quoted at length these passages, so characteristic of
classical Marxism, because they seem to me to provide a clue to
the understanding of Bolshevism and of the relationship between the Russian revolution and the world. The Bolsheviks
grew up in the tradition of which Engels expressed the quintes-
sence; and even after the 'epicentre of revolution' had moved
from Western Europe to Russia they still thought of the establishment of socialism as an international process and not simply
a Russian 'event.' Their own victory was in their eyes a prelude
to world revolution or at least to a European socialist upheaval.
Hindsight tells us that in so far as they expected an imminent
international revolution they were mistaken. But hindsight
may not see the events more clearly than did a bold, even though
partly erroneous, historical foresight. The Bolsheviks started
from the premise that the catastrophe of 1914 had inaugurated
a whole epoch of world wars and revolutions, the epoch of capitalist decline. This premise was historically correct. The next
decades were in fact filled by a gigantic contest between revolution and counter-revolution. In 1918 revolution overthrew the

empires of the Hohenzollerns and Habsburgs and brought into being, if only for a short time, councils of workers' deputies in Berlin, Vienna, Munich, Budapest, and Warsaw. And even after revolution was defeated in Germany, Austria, Hungary, and other countries, the capitalist system did not regain its old stability. It staggered on from crisis to crisis, until the world-wide slump of 1929 brought it to the brink of ruin. The possessing classes first saved their domination by agreeing to economic and political reforms for which generations of socialists had fought in vain before the Russian revolution. Then fascism and Nazism came forward as the saviors of capitalism. Colonial upheavals and the great Chinese revolution of 1925-27 gave to the crisis a new range and depth. And in Europe, after the shadow of the Third Reich had fallen across it, Austria and Spain were shaken by civil wars, and France experienced the stormy class struggles of the Popular Front period. All this indicates how vast were the revolutionary potentialities of the interwar decades. The Second World War again revealed the crisis and disintegration of the social system. In Nazi-occupied Europe people fought not only for their national independence; civil war raged within many an occupied nation. The revolutionary aftermath of the war in France, Italy, and Greece is a matter of historical record. Eastern Europe was transformed by revolution from above. Not since the Napoleonic wars had Europe experienced any comparable social breakdown.

The Bolsheviks understood quite well the epoch in which they had entered upon the stage of world history. It was the epoch of world wars and revolutions. That so many revolutionary efforts have been frustrated or have proved abortive does not invalidate the premise on which they acted. Men engaged in combat do not take defeat for granted before the battle is joined—it is in the actual fighting that the outcome of the struggle is decided. Lenin and his comrades did not as a rule provoke battle arbitrarily—more often than not trials of strength were imposed on them. And revolutionaries may take the view, traditionally held by British soldiers, that they may lose all the battles except the last one, and that in the meantime they have to fight the battles that they have to lose.

Lenin and his followers stood by the universality of the revolution for yet another reason. They saw little or no hope for the achievement of socialism in Russia alone. Isolated from the advanced industrial countries and reduced to her own resources, Russia could not, or not for a very long time, overcome economic scarcity, the low level of her civilization, or the weakness of her working class; she could not prevent the rise of bureaucracy. All Bolsheviks—and this goes even for Stalin—expected at first that Russia would join a European socialist community in which Germany, France, or Britain would take the lead and would help Russia to move towards socialism in a rational and civilized manner, without anything like the sacrifices, the violence, and the social inequality that were to accompany the industrialization of an isolated Soviet Union. As early as 1914 Lenin's watchword was: The United States of Socialist Europe, although later he had his doubts not about the idea itself but about whether it would be properly understood. Then, in 1918, he argued that socialism 'is already a reality in our days; but its two halves are as it were torn asunder: one half, the political conditions for it— the rule of the proletariat exercised through the Soviets—has been created in Russia; while the other half, the industrial and cultural prerequisites, exist in Germany.' To achieve socialism these 'two halves' had to be brought together. If Engels argued against Lafargue that neither the French nor the Germans 'could have all to themselves the glory' of doing away with capitalism, Lenin had not a shred of Lafargue's illusion. He and his comrades knew that the emancipation of the workers could result only from the joint efforts of many nations; and that if the nation-state provided too narrow a framework even for modern capitalism, socialism was quite unthinkable within such a framework. This conviction permeated all Bolshevik thinking and activity until the end of the Lenin era.

Then, in the middle 1920s, the fact of Russia's isolation in the world struck home with a vengeance, and Stalin and Bukharin came forward to expound Socialism in One Country. The Bolsheviks had to take cognizance of the bitter necessity for Russia to 'go it alone' for as long as she had to—that was the rational kernel in the new doctrine which captivated many good internationalists; and with it neither Trotsky nor Zinoviev nor Kamenev had any quarrel.

But the special significance of the new doctrine lay elsewhere, in the fact that it made a virtue out of the necessity, and that it represented a reaction against the universalist conception of the revolution. Arguing from the Soviet Union's isolation, Stalin and Bukharin produced the watchword for a kind of ideological isolationism. They proclaimed that Russia, unaided and unsupported by other nations, could and should not merely advance towards socialism, which was to all Bolsheviks self-evident; but that she could by herself achieve fully fledged socialism—a classless society free from man's domination by man, which was, at best, a pipe dream. They said in effect that, barring war, the fate of the new Soviet society was quite independent of what was going on in the rest of the world; and that socialism could be and was going to be a nationally self-sufficient, closed, autarchic system. To paraphrase Engels, they made of the 'emancipation of the proletariat' a purely Russian event, and by this alone they rendered it impossible. The practical implications were soon to become evident. For over three decades Socialism in One Country was the official canon and the central dogma of Stalinism, imposed in a quasi-ecclesiastical manner upon Party and State. To doubt its truth was blasphemy, and for commiting it, uncounted multitudes of party members and other citizens were punished with excommunication, prison, and death. Up till now, though socialism is supposed to have spread to a dozen countries in the meantime, Socialism in One Country has not yet been stripped of its canonicity.

Behind the idea of a self-sufficient Russian socialism there was the tacit acceptance of the view that the prospects of revolution in the West had faded for good. This undoubtedly reflected a popular mood. After many years of fighting, famine, and frustration the people were desperately weary, and shrugged off the party's customary promises that the international revolution, the great liberating force of the Western proletariat, would soon come to their rescue. The new doctrine held out a different prospect: it assured the people that, even if the Russian revolution were to remain isolated forever, it would still fulfil its promise of socialism and establish the classless society within its own boundaries. 'This is a doctrine of consolation,' Eugene Varga, one of its eminent expounders, confessed in private. It was also, we may add, a doctrine of exaction, for in the name of Socialism in One Country the people were presently asked to give up all civil liberties and bear endless heavy sacrifices and privations. The men of the ruling group, and the bureaucracy at large, had, in addition, their own motives of *Realpolitik* and *raison d'état*. The thinking of any bureaucracy is tied to the nation-state, is shaped by it, and is limited by it. The Bolshevik bureaucracy now descended from the heights of the heroic period of the revolution to the bottomlands of the nation-state; and Stalin led it in the descent. They craved security for themselves and *their* Russia. They strove to preserve the national and, above all, the international status quo, and to find a stable *modus vivendi* with the great capitalist powers. They were convinced that they could find it in a kind of ideological isolationism, and were anxious to disengage the Soviet Union from the class struggles and the social conflicts in the outside world. In proclaiming Socialism in One Country, Stalin in effect told the bourgeois West that he was not vitally interested in socialism in other countries. And the bourgeois West understood him well, even though it wondered whether to take him on trust. During the great struggle between Stalin and Trotsky, most of our statesmen and leaders of opinion held that the West's interest would best be served if Stalin won. He stood for moderation and peaceful co-existence.

However, Stalinism could not easily disentangle itself from the class struggles and the social conflicts in the outside world. It was burdened with a revolutionary heritage which it could neither scrap nor jettison. The headquarters of the Communist International were in Moscow; and the International was the embodiment of the Bolsheviks' earlier allegiance to universal revolution. For a very long time Stalin could not afford to disband the Comintern—he dared the *coup* only in 1943. Meanwhile he did what he could to adapt it to his purpose. He tamed it. He turned it into an auxiliary of his diplomacy, or, as Trotsky once put it, he transformed the foreign Communist parties, from the 'vanguards of world revolution,' into pacifist frontier-guards of the Soviet Union. The Communist parties consented in fact to minister to the diplomatic interests and to the national egoism of the 'workers' first State,' because it had been the workers' first state. They did not have the courage to insist on their own independence even though if they had done so they would have saved their political dignity and revolutionary efficacy. They thus involved themselves in a suicidal equivocation: an International operating as a mere agent of Socialism in One Country was a pathetic contradiction in terms.

The Stalinist search for national security within the framework of the international status quo might have made some sense if the status quo had been inherently stable. But this was not the case. Nothing could have been more precarious than the social equilibrium and the international balance of power of the interwar decades. The social equilibrium was catastrophically upset by the great slump of 1929. The military and diplomatic balance was disrupted by Germany's recovery from the defeat of 1918 and her determination to overthrow the system based on the Treaty of Versailles. Russia could not insulate herself from the shocks these developments produced. Yet what Stalin, his diplomacy, and his tamed Comintern did was to try to insulate her, and even to forestall the shocks and to hold off or mitigate the conflicts abroad into which she might be drawn. The great ruthless dictator, the supposed master of *Realpolitik*, was in fact the King Canute of our century, bidding the waves of revolution, counter-revolution, and war to stand still. In view of the tremendous authority Stalin exercised over world communism, an authority backed by the whole power and prestige of the Soviet Union, his attitude and policy did, of course, a great deal to shape world history in a fateful epoch. No one can say what the West, or what the world at large, would have looked like by now if the labour movement outside the Soviet Union had followed its own interests and traditions and not allowed external influence, Stalinist or otherwise, to interfere with the rhythm and direction of its own development. Perhaps the advanced nations of the West might have achieved their socialist revolution by now; or they might have come much closer to it than they are to-day.

I do not think that the defeats of revolution and socialism in the West were as inevitable as they may now appear to have been. I do not think that they have all been caused by objective circumstances, that is by the inherent 'soundness' of our Western society. At least some of the major reverses of socialism have been due to subjective factors, to the unsoundness of the policies promoted by men and parties who were supposed to be the champions of socialism. The Marxist predictions about class struggle in capitalism were not as wide of the mark as they may now seem, except in so far as Marx, Engels, and Lenin did not reckon with Stalinism and its international consequences.

A major example, one of many that could be adduced, may be given as illustration. Any student of recent history will be struck and perhaps baffled by the utter impassivity and indifference with which in the early 1930s Moscow viewed the rise of Nazism. Stalin, his advisers, and his propagandists showed at that time not the slightest awareness of what was coming. They had no inkling of the gathering force and destructive dynamism of the Nazi movement. From 1929 to 1933 they prompted the German Communist Party to commit a long series of fatal blunders, blunders which made it all too easy for Hitler to seize power. Now, was Hitler's triumph in 1933 really inevitable? Did objective circumstances make it so? Or could the German labour movement have prevented it? Before trying to answer these questions we have to consider the fact that in 1933 that movement surrendered all its positions to Hitler without a struggle. This is true of both parties, the Social Democrats who controlled the trade unions and had an electoral following of over eight million people, and the Communists who had a following of over five million. The most vigorous and militant elements of the movement were in the Communist Party. Because of their own political weight, and because of the influence their conduct exercised on the more inert mass of Social Democrats, their behaviour in the crisis was of the utmost importance. Yet the Communist Party deliberately and systematically played down the Nazi danger and told the workers that the Social Democrats or 'Social-fascists,' not the Nazis, were the chief enemy on whom they ought to 'concentrate all fire.' The leaders of both parties, the Social Democrats and the Communists, refused even to contemplate the idea of any common action against Nazism. There was no objective reason why they should behave in this way. Their surrender was not inevitable. Hitler's easy victory in 1933 was not inevitable. And Stalin and the Soviet party had no real interest whatsoever in sponsoring the policy of surrender and persisting in it. Their apathy and indifference in the face of rising Nazism resulted solely from the isolationist temper of Stalinism, from its desire to keep the Soviet Union out of any entanglement in any major conflict abroad. Playing for safety, Stalin ruled out any Communist move in Germany that might have led to a confrontation, and possibly to civil war, between the German left and Nazism. Pursuing the mirage of security within the international status quo, the mirage of Socialism in One Country, Stalinism caused the defeat of socialism in many other countries and exposed the Soviet Union to mortal peril. Some of us argued in those years, well before 1933, that a Nazi government meant world war and invasion of the Soviet Union; that it was the duty of the German left to bar Hitler's road to power; that it had a fair chance of succeeding in this; and that even if it were to fail, it should go down fighting rather than passively accept the prospect of its own annihilation by the Nazis. We were decried in Moscow as panic-mongers, war-mongers, and enemies of the German proletariat and of the Soviet Union.

The surrender of 1933 was the most crushing defeat Marxism ever suffered, a defeat which was to be deepened by later events and later Stalinist policies, a defeat from which the German and the European labour movements have not yet recovered. If the German left, and above all the German Communist Party, had not allowed itself to be goaded into capitulation, if it had had the sense to fight for its life, there might never have been a Third Reich and a Second World War. The Soviet Union might not have lost 20 million dead on the battlefields. The smoke from the Auschwitz gas chambers might not have blackened the record of our civilization. And meanwhile, Germany might perhaps have become a workers' state.

One could give other examples of how the Stalinist obsession with security led to catastrophic insecurity, and how ideological isolationism invariably aggravated the Soviet Union's isolation, which, of course, drove Soviet policy into ever deeper isolationism. The vicious circle is reproduced at almost every stage of Stalinist and even post-Stalinist diplomacy, whenever the Soviet *raison d'état* has imposed itself on the policy of an important sector of the Western labour movement. This was the case with the Popular Front in France, with the Spanish Civil War, and with the repercussions of the Nazi-Soviet Pact of 1939-41. In all these instances it was not so much the inherent strength of Western capitalism as the national egoism of Stalin's policy that inflicted defeat after defeat on the forces of socialism in the West; and each of these defeats was a setback for the Soviet Union as well.

The Second World War and the Nazi invasion drove the Soviet Union out of its isolation. Once again the emancipation of the workers—and, of course, the liberation of Europe from Nazi domination—could 'only be an international event.' Not only the armies of the great Powers waged the war. Guerillas, partisans, and resisters of many nations did so as well. An international civil war, with tremendous social revolutionary potentialities, unfolded within the world war. Stalinism, however, went on clinging to conventional security, *raison d'état*, and sacred national egoism. It fought the war as a 'Fatherland War,' another 1812, not as a European civil war. It would not confront Nazism with the idea of international socialism and revolution. Stalin did not believe that that idea would inspire his armies to fight, or that it could infect and disintegrate the enemy's armies, as it had done during the wars of intervention. Moreover, he prompted the various Communist-led resistance movements in Europe to fight solely for national liberation, not for socialism. In part he was actuated by the desire to preserve the Grand Alliance; he assumed correctly that if the war threatened to turn into a European revolution, Churchill and Roosevelt would contract out of the alliance. In part, however, he himself was afraid of the revolutionary turmoil, which might have upset the precarious social-political balance within the Soviet Union on which his autocracy rested. He was determined to emerge from the gigantic upheaval with Socialism in One Country and with his autocracy intact. Yet the logic of the war turned against his isolationist ideology. He had to send his armies into a dozen foreign countries; and even while they marched under the Fatherland banners these were still Red Armies, which would not be easily persuaded that their victory, so dearly bought, should end in the restoration of capitalism in all the lands they freed from Nazi occupation. The revolutionary aftermath of the war was there. How to keep it under control, and how to reduce it to a minimum was, at Teheran and Yalta, the common preoccupation of

F

Stalin, Roosevelt, and Churchill. They tackled the problems of
the alliance in the spirit of conventional diplomacy and shared
out and delineated their respective spheres of influence.

We need not here go into the complicated conflicts that en-
sued even before the end of hostilities and ushered in the cold
war. Suffice it to say that, even while the Soviet Union was involved as never before in the affairs of so many countries, and
while Stalin had to secure the fruits of victory, the Soviet Union's predominance in Eastern Europe, by quasi-revolutionary
methods, Stalinism remained true to its national narrow-mindedness. The revolution in Eastern Europe was not to be the
'international event brought about by the joint efforts of the
proletariat of many nations.' It was imposed from above by
the occupying Power and its agents. And the so-called People's
Democracies were to be merely the defensive *glacis* of Socialism
in One Country. In Western Europe bourgeois rule, battered
and discredited, was restored in accordance with the pacts of
Yalta and Teheran; and the Communist parties there assisted
in the restoration, participating in de Gaulle's and Gaspari's
postwar governments, helping to disarm the Resistance, and
curbing the restive radicalism of the working classes. In this way
the revolutionary potentialities of the postwar period were realized, but distorted in the realization, all over Eastern Europe;
and they were nullified in Western Europe. Thus Stalinism
worked to produce a stalemate in the class struggle which was to
enable diplomacy to secure the 'peaceful co-existence of the opposed social systems.' Once again Stalin sought to obtain national security on the basis of the international status quo, that
is, of the division of zones agreed upon at Teheran and Yalta.
However, diplomacy could not remove all the big bones of con-
tention that the masters of Teheran and Yalta had strewn along
the boundaries of their zones; nor was it able to cope with the
unfamiliar perils of the nuclear age. And so the world was left
to shiver in the bleak blasts of the cold war, which was but a

depraved form of the class struggle waged by the great Powers. One is again reminded of Engels's warning: 'Exclusive French leadership of the bourgeois revolution led—you know where—to Napoleon, to conquest, and to invasion by the Holy Alliance.' More than once exclusive Russian leadership in the socialist revolution was ominously close to producing the same results.

However, the epoch of exclusive Russian leadership was coming to an end. The revolutionary aftermath of the war had not been brought under complete control, after all. The Yugoslavs defied the Russian leadership; and the victorious Chinese revolution confronted it implicitly with a huge challenge. Yet even the spread of revolution did not cure Stalinist policy of its national egoism and isolationism; and to these ills the policy of Stalin's successors still remains the heir. Even if the concept of Socialism in One Country has long since lost all relevance, the mood behind it, and the way of thinking and the style of political action inspired by it have survived.

Yet another aspect of the Soviet Union's impact on the social and political life of the West may now be briefly considered. In the first years after 1917 the message of the October revolution aroused a deep response in the Western labour movement. In 1920, for instance, Congresses of the French and Italian Socialist parties and of the German Independent Socialist Party, then the most influential body on the German left, voted by large majorities to join the Communist International. Even in conservative Britain the dockers of London, led by Ernest Bevin, expressed their sympathy with the new Russia by refusing to load munitions destined for Polish armies fighting against the Soviets. It looked as if the Western labour movement had raised itself, under the inspiration of the Russian revolution, from the slough to which it had sunk in 1914. During the Second World War again, the battle of Stalingrad lifted Nazi-occupied Europe from the depths of despair and inspired the Resistance with confidence in victory and fresh socialist hope. But on balance, over this half-century, the example of the Soviet Union, far from stimulating the labour movements of the West, has deterred them from pursuing their socialist aspirations.

Paradoxically, a major reason for this was that the workers saw the Russian revolution as the first great historic test of socialism. They were not aware of the tragic handicaps with which the Soviet Union was burdened. No matter what some Marxist theorists said about these handicaps, no matter how cogently they argued that a free and classless society could not come into being in one poverty-stricken and semi-barbarous country, to the mass of our workers these were niceties of abstract theory. To them socialism in Russia was now a matter not of theoretical speculation but of practical experience. Clearly, it was not in the Soviet interest to encourage exaggerated hopes. Soviet leaders, aware of their responsibility, would have conscientiously explained the position, as Lenin used to do; and they would have made it clear that even the great achievements of the Soviet Union were and could be only preliminaries to socialism, not the real stuff of socialism. They might thus have avoided fostering illusions and prevented subsequent disillusionment; and they might have impressed upon the labour movement of the West its co-responsibility for the isolation and the predicaments of the Soviet Union. Stalin and his associates, however, were too much concerned with national pride and bureaucratic prestige to act in this way. They offered their 'doctrine of consolation,' their myth of Socialism in One Country, to the workers not only of Russia but of the world.

One effect of the spread of this myth was to turn Western communists and socialists into mere spectators. As the Russians were saying that they could well achieve, or even that they had achieved, socialism all by themselves, there seemed nothing left for people in the West to do, except to watch how the Russians were faring. For thirty years or so Stalinist propaganda spoke of the miracles socialism was working in the U.S.S.R. The ardent and the naïve believed. The great majority of Western workers wondered, suspended judgment, or formed negative opinions. Accounts of Soviet poverty, famine, and terror fed the scepticism. The Great Purges and the Stalin cult, zealously defended by all Communist parties, aroused disgust. Then multitudes of American, British, and French soldiers came into contact with their Soviet allies in occupied Germany and Austria; and they drew their conclusions. Finally, in 1956, there was the shock of Khrushchev's revelations. Many millions of Western workers have, over the years, pondered these experiences and have concluded that 'socialism does not work' and that 'revolution leads you nowhere.' Many have sunk into political apathy; and many have reconciled themselves to the social status quo in the West, which the postwar booms and the welfare state have rendered somewhat more tolerable. Intellectuals, who had believed in Soviet socialism, have ended by denouncing the 'God that failed' them. The myth of Socialism in One Country has thus bred an even more deceptive myth—a colossal myth—about the failure of socialism. This double mystification has come to dominate much of Western political thinking and has greatly contributed to the ideological stalemate in which the world still lives half a century after 1917.

The West, however, has hardly any reason to view this outcome with self-righteousness. For when a Russian looks at the record of the West, in its relationship with Russia, what does he find there? The rapacious Peace of Brest Litovsk, the allied armed intervention against the Soviets, the blockade, the *cordon sanitaire*, the prolonged economic and diplomatic boycotts; and then Hitler's invasion and the horrors of Nazi occupation, the long and clever delays by which Russia's allies postponed the opening up of a second front against Hitler, while the Soviet armies were immolating themselves in battle; and, after 1945, the rapid reversal of the alliances, the nuclear blackmail, and the anti-communist frenzy of the cold war. What a record! What a record!

A Marxist must ask why the working classes of the West and

their parties have allowed so much freedom of initiative and action to the governments and establishments who between them were responsible for this record. The historian has to probe the objective circumstances that may have prevented Western socialism, in the course of these fifty years, from intervening radically and from making the West face the Russian revolution in quite a different manner. He has also to make allowance for the adverse effects of the prolonged and exclusive Russian leadership in socialist revolution. But, having carefully considered all objective circumstances and having made all necessary allowances, how will he sum up his conclusions? Engels, speaking about the exclusive French leadership of the bourgeois revolution and its baneful consequences, and having undoubtedly analyzed with care the objective circumstances of the epoch, summed up his view in these few plain and pregnant words: All this, he said, 'was made inevitable because of the stupidity and cowardice of other nations.' Will a future Engels have to pass the same verdict on our epoch?

V

The Soviet Union and the Chinese Revolution

I planned originally to deal in this lecture with the impact of the Russian revolution on the colonial and semi-colonial peoples of the East. But working on this subject, I found it so wide and many-sided as to be almost unmanageable within so small a compass; and so I shall confine myself to one question only, the one on which the theme has come to be focused: the relationship between the Russian and the Chinese revolutions.

The Chinese revolution is in a sense a child of the Russian. I know that some Sinologues will vehemently object to this statement; and I readily admit that their objections are valid within certain limits. Obviously, an historic phenomenon of this magnitude has its deepest roots in its own country, in the conditions of the society of which it is the product. This needs to be strongly emphasized, especially because until quite recently it was customary in the West to treat Chinese communism as something of a Russian puppet. But we should not, on the other hand, treat it as a movement closed within itself, which can be understood *only* in terms of its national environment. We must not allow the Great Wall to dominate our own thinking about the Chinese revolution. Earlier I tried to trace the many filiations between the Russian revolution and the intellectual and political history of Western Europe. I quoted to you Lenin's great acknowledgment of the debt the Russian revolution owed to the West, and Trotsky's words about Europe's 'export of its most advanced ideology to Russia.' Now, the impact of the Russian revolution on China was incomparably more direct and powerful than that of Western Europe on revolutionary Russia.

The Russian revolution triumphed at a moment when the Chinese revolution was in an impasse. When the Chinese overthrew the Manchu dynasty in 1911, they attempted to solve their national problem by means of a purely bourgeois revolution. The attempt failed. China was proclaimed a republic; but her great social and political issues remained unresolved; and they were presently aggravated. The nation sank ever deeper into dependence on foreign powers; the warlords and *compradores* tore it to pieces; and the peasantry, destitute and oppressed, had no chance of changing or improving the condition in which it lived. The purely bourgeois revolution had demonstrated its impotence; and no one was more conscious of this than Sun Yat-sen, its leader. Then, in 1919, came the great national protest against the Treaty of Versailles and the movement against the perpetuation of China's subjection to the great powers. This was still an attempt to revive the 'purely' bourgeois revolution, although it was inspired by Chen Tu-hsiu, the future founder of the Chinese Communist Party. That movement too reached a dead end. In the next year a crucial event occurred: from Moscow the Second Congress of the International called on the colonial and semi-colonial peoples of the East to rise or to prepare for revolution. The great 'import' of Bolshevik ideology to China began; and this was soon to be followed by the importation of Russian military skill and technology. Russia had by her example shown China the way out of the impasse: China too had to go beyond the purely bourgeois revolution. Anti-imperialism, redistribution of the land, the hegemonic role of the industrial workers in revolution, the formation of a Communist Party, and a close alliance with the Soviet Union—these were the new prospects that suddenly opened before Chinese radicals. Even Sun Yat-sen subscribed to some of these new aims, though not without trepidation.

Until then Marxism had exercised almost no influence in China. A few disjointed ideas of Fabian and Methodist social-ism had come down in a trickle to the intelligentsia of Shanghai, Canton, and Peking. But it was only in 1921, seventy-three years after its original publication, that the *Communist Manifesto* appeared in Chinese for the first time.[1] Western European Marxism, with its concentration on the class struggle in the advanced industrial countries, could hardly strike any chord in the radical intelligentsia of a semi-colonial peasant nation. It was from the Russians, and in the Russian version, that the Chinese took their Marxism. As Mr. E. H. Carr rightly points out in his great *History of the Soviet Union*, it was Lenin who for the first time formulated a Marxist programme of action that was immediately relevant to the peoples of the East. He was able to do this because of his *Narodnik*-like sensitivity to the problems of the peasantry, and because of his wholly original grasp of the significance of the anti-imperialist struggle.

Bolshevism faced both West and East. We have seen that facing the West and considering the prospects of socialism there, Lenin insisted that the nation-state formed too narrow a base for socialist transformation. Up to 1924 all the great manifestoes of the Communist International culminated in a call for the Socialist United States of Europe. In the East, however, the situation was different. Its peoples still lived in the pre-industrial and even pre-bourgeois epoch, fragmented by quasi-feudal particularisms, tribal patriarchalism, caste systems, and warlordism. If for the West the nation-state, the great achievement of the past, was

---

[1] A reviewer of an essay on Maoism, included in my *Ironies of History*, recalls, in *The Times Literary Supplement*, that excerpts from the *Manifesto* had been translated into Chinese, and apparently published in a small periodical, in the first decade of this century. The fact remains that Chinese readers of Mao Tse-tung's generation, and Mao himself, could not read the *Manifesto* in extenso until 1921.

already an obstacle to progress, for the peoples of the East this
achievement still lay in the future and was an essential condition
of progress. But if in the West the modern nation-state was the
product of bourgeois revolution, the East had to go beyond that
revolution in order to attain it. This was the great new lesson
Moscow broadcast in the early 1920s. Even so, Moscow did not
view the Chinese or any other Eastern revolution as a purely
national struggle, but as part of an international process; and it
still attributed to the proletarian socialist revolution of the West
the leading part in the world-wide struggle. Bolshevism projected
its own experience upon the world scene. In Russia the revolution had taken place in both town and country; but the directing
initiative, intelligence, and will had come from the town; and
this, the Bolsheviks thought, would repeat itself on a global
scale, where the industrial West was the 'town' writ large, while
the undeveloped East was the 'country.'

The next Chinese revolution, which occurred in the years
1925-27, seemed to confirm this expectation. Britain was at that
time shaken by the greatest class struggles in her history, the long-
est and the most stubborn miners' strike on record and the General Strike of 1926. In China the alignment of the social forces
broadly resembled the Russian pattern: the country was ablaze
with agrarian revolt; but the urban workers were the driving force
of the revolution. It is necessary to recall this important, but now
forgotten or ignored, fact. Much of recent Chinese history has,
unfortunately, been rewritten by Maoists and Stalinists alike;
and not only have many historic personalities been turned into
Orwellian unpersons, but an entire social class—the Chinese industrial proletariat of the 1920s—has been deleted from the historical record and turned into an unclass. We shall presently see
why this has happened.

The fate of the revolution of the 1920s was tragic enough. Not
only was it defeated; but before its defeat it had been driven
back into the impasse of the purely bourgeois revolution, from
which Leninism had just shown the way out. Stalin and his as-

sociates and agents in China drove it back there. We in the West do not have to rely on Stalinist or Maoist 'rewrites' of history; so I assume that you are familiar with the broad outline of the events; and I shall only recall here that Stalin's policy centred on the idea that the Chinese revolution must have purely bourgeois objectives and that it should be based on the so-called 'bloc of four classes.' In fact, Moscow forced the reluctant Chinese communists to submit unconditionally to the direction and discipline of the Kuomintang; to accept General Chiang Kai-shek as the national leader and hero; to refrain from encouraging agrarian revolts; and finally, in 1927, to disarm the insurgent workers in the cities. In this way the first great, victorious proletarian uprising in Asia, the Commune of Shanghai, was suppressed. This was followed by a wholesale massacre of communists and insurgent workers and by the debacle of the revolution.

It has been argued that, regardless of Stalin's policy, the revolution of 1925-27 was doomed anyhow, because of its inherent 'immaturity.' The historian cannot in a post mortem disentangle the objective causes of an event like this from the subjective ones, from men's policies and moves; he cannot say which of these factors decided the outcome of the struggle. The fact is that whether the defeat of the revolution was inevitable in 1927 or not, Stalinism did all it could to make it so. In the East no less than in the West, Stalinist policy was actuated by the fear of destroying or upsetting the status quo, and by the desire to avoid deep involvement in grave social conflicts abroad that might lead to 'international complications.' In the East, no less than in the West, Stalinism worked to produce a stalemate in the class struggle.

In China, however, a stalemate was impossible. The revolution had been crushed in the cities; but the counter-revolution was unable to consolidate its victory. The social structure of the country was shattered. The peasant revolts continued. The regime of the Kuomintang was rickety and corrupt. And then, in the course of fifteen years, the Japanese invasion dealt blow after blow to the social structure and the political regime. Nothing could arrest the process of decomposition.

The defeat of 1927, however, and subsequent events set the scene for a revolution very different from that of the 1920s, and very different also from the Russian pattern of 1905 and 1917. In the late 1920s, after the massacre of its members, the Communist Party found it extremely difficult to rebuild its urban strongholds. In the 1930s, the Japanese, having conquered coastal China, embarked upon forcible de-industrialization of the occupied cities, dismantled the factories, and thus caused a dispersal of the urban workers. Even before that, however, Mao urged the Communist Party to turn its back upon the cities and to invest all its energies in partisan warfare, which was to be waged in the rural areas where the peasantry was in uproar. His political strategy was summed up, after many years, in the celebrated phrase that in China the revolution must be carried not from town to country, but from country to town.

Was this strategy a stroke of political genius? Or was it, perhaps, an adventurer's desperate gamble? Its eventual success makes it appear to have been the former. But in the light of the circumstances of the time it was indeed a dubious gamble. Stalinist Moscow treated it for a long time as a harmless aberration which did not even merit excommunication as a heresy. Incidentally, Mao repaid this indulgence by observing outwardly all the devotions of the Stalin cult. As Stalin saw it, Mao's partisans, though they came to control considerable rural areas, had no chance whatsoever of carrying the revolution from country to town and of overthrowing the Kuomintang. Stalin was glad to use them as a bargaining counter in his dealings with Chiang Kai-shek; and so he offered them a little cheap publicity in the newspapers of the Comintern, but otherwise gave them no assistance. He looked upon Mao as upon a queer pawn on his chessboard, placed in one of its less important corners.

And, in truth, Mao's strategy needed for its success an extraordinary combination or coincidence of circumstances, such as he neither foresaw nor could have foreseen. It took fifteen years of Japanese invasion and occupation, fifteen years during which China was dismembered and plunged in chaos; and it took a world war and Japan's defeat, to enable Mao's partisans to survive and gain strength; and to bring the Kuomintang to that point of collapse at which a peasant army could push it over. Normally, in our epoch—and this had been so even in undeveloped China—the town dominates the country economically, administratively, and militarily to such an extent that attempts to carry revolution from country to town are doomed beforehand. But in 1948 and 1949, when the partisans entered Nanking, Tiensin, Shanghai, Canton, and Peking they moved into a virtual vacuum. The Kuomintang's disintegration was complete. This is what Stalin failed to grasp even in 1948, when in vain he urged Mao to make peace with Chiang Kai-shek and agree to the incorporation of the partisans in Chiang's army. Afraid once again of 'complications'—of massive American intervention in Far Eastern areas adjacent to Soviet frontiers—Stalin was still—in 1948!—trying to recapture the Chinese status quo of 1928.

In the meantime the character of the revolution and the outlook of Chinese communism had changed radically. Mao's party bore, in ideology and organization, little resemblance either to Lenin's party or to Stalin's. Lenin's party had its roots deep in the working class. Mao's was based almost exclusively on the peasantry. The Bolsheviks had grown up within a multi-party system which had existed, half-submerged, in Tsarist Russia; and they had been accustomed to the give and take of intense controversy with their opponents, Mensheviks, Social Revolutionaries, Liberals, and others. The Maoists, living for over twenty years in complete isolation, entrenched in their mountain fastnesses, caves, and villages, had become wholly introverted. They had no Mensheviks or Social Revolutionaries to confront in direct debate. Their polemics against the Kuomintang were in the nature of war propaganda that had to be conducted against an enemy rather than an ideological controversy with a serious opponent. The party cadres formed the commanding corps of the partisans. Everything in their life was subordinated to the imperative needs of an armed contest. The organization, the discipline, the habits of thought, the day-to-day conduct of affairs were militarized. Unconventional and revolutionary though their militarism was, it stood in striking contrast to the predominantly civilian character of the Bolshevik Party. If Bolshevism had become monolithic through a long series of painful political and moral crises, after the suppression of many internal oppositions, Maoism had little to suppress in its own ranks; its monolithic character was a natural and unconstrained growth. And so, although outwardly Maoism resembled Stalinism, the similarity concealed deep differences.

Sinologues often compare Mao's partisans with the Chinese peasant armies that over the ages rose and overthrew dynasties to put their own leaders on the throne. No doubt, the partisans are in some ways descendants of those armies. In China too the past has refracted itself in the revolution—the past with its traditions of the Mandarinate as well as of the peasant risings. If Stalinism was the amalgam of Marxism with the savage barbarism of the old Russia, Maoism may be considered as an amalgam of Leninism with China's primitive patriarchalism and ancestral cults. Maoism is, in any case, far more deeply permeated by native custom and habit than the urban communism of the 1920s had been. Even a literary comparison of the writings of Mao and Chen Tu-hsiu, Mao's predecessor in the party leadership, reveals the difference: Mao's idiom is far more archaic than Chen Tu-hsiu's, whose language was closer to that of the European, especially the Russian, Marxists of the pre-Stalin era. (Not for nothing does Mao compose his poems in the classical Mandarin style.)

Great though the power of the past over the present may be, however, we need not exaggerate it. In China as in Russia, the amalgam of a modern revolutionary ideology with primordial native tradition is the phenomenon of an epoch of transition. Here and there society has been in the throes of a transformation which reduces or destroys the force of custom and habit. Here and there the rulers have used tradition for purposes which uproot the traditional way of life. We have seen how industrialization, urbanization, and mass education render the Stalinist amalgam inacceptable to Soviet society; and it may be assumed that in this, if in nothing else, the Soviet Union prefigures the image of China's not too remote future.

In any case, Mao's partisans, unlike the old rebellious peasant armies, have not left the patriarchal structure of Chinese society intact. They were the agents of a modern bourgeois revolution which could not be contained within bourgeois limits; and they initiated a socialist revolution. They produced in fact the second great act of the international upheaval that had begun in Russia in 1917.

How was it that they were able to produce it? In Russia the double revolution was the outcome of an Homeric struggle waged primarily by the industrial workers, who were led by their genuine socialist vanguard. Mao's party, we know, had no connexion with any industrial proletariat; and the latter played no significant part in the events of 1948-49. The peasantry stood for the redistribution of the land and private property. The so-called national bourgeoisie, disheartened and demoralized by the Kuomintang's corruption and disintegration, entertained the hope that Maoism would not go beyond the limits of bourgeois revolution. To sum up, in 1948-49 no basic social class in China strove to establish socialism.

In embarking upon the socialist revolution the Maoists enacted the role which the Bolsheviks had assumed only some years after 1917, that of trustees and guardians of an almost nonexistent industrial working class. In so far as they enjoyed the peasantry's support, the Maoists were not an isolated revolutionary elite, without any social class behind them. But the peasantry, its individualism focused on the rural economy, was, at best, indifferent to what was happening in the town.

In going far beyond the peasantry's horizon, the Maoists were actuated by at least three motives: (a) the ideological commitments into which they had entered in their early, formative years; (b) considerations of national interest; and (c) imperatives of international security. In their young years, while they underwent the influence of the Leninist school of thought, they had absorbed the ideas of proletarian socialism. During the decades of their immersion in rural China they had little or no use for those ideas, and they identified themselves with the peasantry's individualism. But, having re-entered the cities as China's rulers, they could not allow themselves to be guided just by that individualism, which, translated into urban terms, meant private enterprise in industry and trade. They were struggling to unify the nation, to create a centralized government, to build a modern nation-state. They could not base it on a stunted native capitalism vulnerable to Western pressures. Nationalized industry and banking provided a far safer foundation for national independence and a unitary state, for industrialization and China's re-emergence as a great power. Although in theory these objectives were compatible with a purely bourgeois revolution, a semi-colonial nation could not, in this century, attain them by bourgeois means. (Characteristically, Mao did not expropriate the capitalists without compensation: he has paid them to this day an indemnity in the form of long-term dividends, and has accorded them managerial posts in the economy. This fact, however, does not by itself detract from the socialist character of the revolution.) Finally, considerations of international security drove the new China towards the Soviet Union. Up to the moment of victory the Maoists had fought Kuomintang armies which were 'advised' by American generals and equipped with American weapons; occasionally, they had to do battle against American Marines as well. The United States upheld Chiang as the counter-revolutionary Pretender. The cold war was rising to its pitch; and the world was dividing into two blocs. In these circumstances China's security lay in a close alliance with the Soviet Union and in Soviet economic aid; and this necessitated the adjustment of her social and political structure to that of the Soviet Union.

It was not easy for the new China to achieve close alliance with the U.S.S.R. The relations between the two communist powers were strained and surrounded by ambiguity from the outset. The national egoism of Stalin's government was the major cause of the strains. Even if Mao and his comrades were willing to forget how Stalin had used them in the 1920s, and how he had then treated the partisans and obstructed their final bid for power, they could not easily reconcile themselves to the position the Russians held in the Far East since Japan's defeat. The Russians had re-established their predominance in Manchuria; they held the Far Eastern Railway and Port Arthur; and they had dismantled and carried away as 'war booty' the industrial plant of Manchuria—that province was then China's only industrial base, on which her economic development depended. Nor did Moscow show any sign of willingness to relinquish its hold on Soviet Mongolia, although in the past all Soviet leaders had given many solemn pledges that one day, when the revolution had won in China, the whole of Mongolia would be united in a single republic federated with China. In all this there were the makings of a conflict far graver than that into which Stalin and Tito had just plunged, a conflict as grave as that which was to turn Khrushchev and Mao against each other a decade later. However, in 1950 neither Stalin nor Mao could afford to fall out. Stalin was wary of driving the Maoists and the Titoists into a common front; and Mao was so anxious to obtain Soviet good will and assistance that he struck a compromise with Stalin and clinched the alliance. The Soviet Union acted as the guarantor of the Chinese revolution and of its socialist character.

The Chinese revolution was, of course, fraught with all the contradictions which troubled the Russian revolution, those be-

G

tween its bourgeois and its socialist aspects and those inherent in any attempt to establish socialism in an undeveloped country. Similar circumstances produced similar results. Hence, despite their differences, the affinity between Maoism and Stalinism. Both acted within the single-party system, as holders of a power monopoly, and as guardians and trustees of the socialist interest, although Mao, having had no real experience of a multi-party system and no tradition of European Marxism behind him, acted that role with far less guilt and with far greater ease than Stalin. And Maoism, like Stalinism, reflected the backwardness of its native environment, which it would take the revolution a very long time to digest and overcome.

The alliance, for all its ambiguity, brought vital benefits to both partners. Stalin had obtained not only the Chinese accession to the principle of exclusive Soviet leadership in the socialist camp; he also gained, through special Soviet-Chinese joint stock companies, a direct influence on the conduct of China's economic and political affairs. These mixed companies could not but hurt the susceptibilities of many Chinese, to whom they looked like new versions of old-fashioned Western concessions. Nevertheless, thanks to Soviet aid, the new China was not as isolated in the world as Bolshevik Russia had been in the years after 1917. The Western blockade could not impose on her the hardships it had once imposed on Russia. China was not at the outset reduced to her own desperately inadequate resources. Soviet engineering and scientific-managerial advice and Soviet training of Chinese specialists and workers eased the start of China's industrialization, lightened for her the burden of primitive accumulation, and speeded up her 'take off.' Consequently, China did not have to pay the high price for pioneering in socialism that Russia had paid, even though the Chinese started from far lower levels of economic and cultural development. Mao's government did not have to cut as deeply into the peasantry's income as Stalin's did, in order to provide the sinews of industrialization; nor did it have to keep the urban consumers on such short rations. These circumstances (and others which I cannot go into here) account for the fact that in the first decade of the revolution, social and political relations, especially those between town and country, were less tense in China than they had been in Russia.

Nothing seemed to stand in the way of an even closer association between the two powers, especially when, after Stalin's death, his successors disbanded the joint stock companies, renounced direct control, and waived most of the humiliating conditions that Stalin had attached to aid. Indeed, the time seemed auspicious for the establishment of something like a socialist commonwealth stretching from the seas of China to the Elbe. In such a commonwealth one-third of mankind would have jointly planned its economic and social development on the basis of a broad rational division of labour and of an intensive exchange of goods and services. Socialism might at last have begun to turn into 'an international event.'

So ambitious an undertaking would, no doubt, have met with a host of difficulties, arising out of the huge discrepancies between the economic structures and standards of living and between the levels of civilization and the national traditions of the many participating nations. The cleavage between the haves and the have-nots, the most burdensome part of the legacy that socialist revolution inherits from the past, would have made itself felt in any case. The have-nots, the Chinese in the first instance, were bound to press for an equalization of the economic levels and standards of living within the commonwealth; and their demands could not but clash with rising consumer expectations in the Soviet Union, Czechoslovakia, and East Germany. But these should not have been insuperable obstacles to a serious socialist attempt to transcend the nation-state economically. A broad division of labour and intensive exchange were sure to yield considerable advantages to all members of the commonwealth, to economize resources, to save energies, and to create new margins of wealth and new economic elbow room for all.

Nothing stood in the way of such a design except the inertia
of national self-sufficiency and bureaucratic arrogance. In de-
scribing how the thinking of any bureaucracy is tied to the nation-state, is shaped by it and is limited by it, I said earlier that
even the spread of revolution could not cure Stalinist policy of
its national egoism and ideological isolationism; and that to
these ills the policy of Stalin's successors still remains the heir.
Even if the concept of Socialism in One Country has long since
lost all relevance, the mood behind it, and the way of thinking
and the style of political action inspired by it have survived. Nowhere has this shown itself more strikingly than in Russo-
Chinese relations. I shall refer here to only one event in that
sphere, the sudden cancellation by Khrushchev's government, in
July 1960, of all economic aid to China and the recall from
China of all Soviet specialists, technicians, and engineers. The
blow this dealt to China was probably far more cruel than had
been, say, the brief and violent impact of Soviet armed intervention in Hungary. As the specialists and engineers had been
ordered to deprive the Chinese of all Soviet construction plans,
blueprints, and patents, a vast number of Chinese industrial en-
terprises was at a stroke brought to a standstill. The Chinese had
invested heavily in the factories and plants under construction;
these investments were frozen. Masses of half-installed machinery and unfinished buildings were left to rust and rot. For a
poverty-stricken nation, only beginning to equip itself, this was
a crippling loss. For about five years China's industrialization
was interrupted; it was slowed down for a much longer period.
Millions of workers were condemned to idleness and privations
and had to trek back to the villages at a time when these were
suffering from floods, droughts, and poor harvests. I cannot help
recalling in this context the extraordinary premonition with
which Lenin, in 1922, in one of his last writings, worried about
the effect that the actions of the 'dzerzhymorda—the Great Russian chauvinist and bureaucratic bully,' might one day have
'among those hundreds of millions of the peoples of Asia who

will in the near future move to the forefront of the historic stage.'

The Maoists have repaid the Russians in their own coin, the coin of national egotism. What we have heard from China ever since has been less and less the rational argument in the controversy over the ends and means of socialism, and more and more the cry of offended and enraged national pride, the cry of the wounded and humiliated. The traumatic shock of 1960 has stirred and brought out of the Maoists all their long pent-up and suppressed resentments against the Russians. It has also forced out of them some of their negative character traits, especially their inveterate Oriental conceit and their contempt for the West, as part of which they have come to see the Soviet Union.

At the heart of the conflict lie the different attitudes of the two powers towards the international status quo. The Russians have continued all these years their old search for national security within the international status quo. It has been, I trust, sufficiently demonstrated that this policy has not been an innovation of Stalin's successors; it has not been that feat of 'Khrushchevite revisionism' that the Maoists denounce. The revisionism is Stalinist in origin; it goes back to the 1920s and to Socialism in One Country. Ever since then Soviet policy has sought to avoid at all cost any deep and risky involvement in the class struggles and social and political conflicts of the outside world. This has been, amid all its varying motives and amid all the changing circumstances of the times, its one constant preoccupation. To it, over twenty years, Stalin had subordinated the strategy and tactics of the Comintern; and then, in the period between 1943 and 1953, all the interests of all Communist parties. In relation to China, Stalin beat all records of 'revisionism,' first in 1927 and then in 1948. In his pursuit of security, he tried as a rule to preserve, and even to stabilize, any existing international balance of power. As he operated in an epoch of violent dislocation and change, he had to adjust his policy to an ever new status quo; and he did so again and again in an essentially conservative manner. In the 1930s he adjusted his policy, and that of the Popular Fronts, to the defence of the Versailles system, when the latter was threatened by Nazism. Between 1939 and 1941 he 'adjusted' himself to the predominance of the Third Reich in Europe. And, finally, he geared his policy to the preservation of the status quo created by the Yalta and Postdam pacts. It is still this status quo, or what has survived of it, that Stalin's successors seek to shore up against the forces disrupting it from inside.

Yet, to the new China this status quo is necessarily unacceptable. Dating back from the time before the Chinese revolution, it was based on the implicit acknowledgment of American predominance in the Pacific area. It does not take into account the Chinese revolution and its consequences. This is the status quo under which China remains the outlaw of international diplomacy; under which she is excluded from the United Nations, blockaded by American fleets and air forces, surrounded by American military bases, and subjected to economic boycott. Moscow, invoking the dangers of nuclear war, is anxious to stabilize this status quo, if need be by imposing a tacit standstill on class struggle and anti-imperialist 'wars of liberation.' China has every motive to encourage, within limits, those forces in Asia and elsewhere that are hostile to the status quo. She has no interest in imposing any standstill on class struggle and wars of liberation. Hence the basic incompatibility of Russian and Chinese policies. Hence the loud quarrel, partly real but partly spurious, about revisionism. Hence the accusation that the Russians, when they seek an accommodation with the West, align themselves with American imperialism against the Chinese revolution and against the peoples that are still oppressed by imperialism. Hence the final Chinese challenge to the Russian leadership of the 'socialist camp,' and the Maoist claim to leadership.

Yet two souls seem to dwell in Maoism: one internationalist, the other seemingly full of Oriental conceit. Their opposition to the status quo and to Russian power politics has induced the Maoists to take up a radical stance and to voice against Moscow the watchwords and slogans of revolutionary-proletarian inter-nationalism. But their own background and experience, their deep immersion in the backwardness of their national milieu, their fresh—yet so old—exalted pride in their nation-state, the prize they have won in their epic struggle, their lack of deep roots in the working class or in any authentically Marxist tradi-tion—all this disposes them towards a national narrow-minded-ness and a sacred egoism quite as intense as the Stalinist; and so they, too, are inclined to subordinate the interests of foreign communist or revolutionary movements to their own *raison d'état* and their own power politics. Even their image of social-ism bears the Stalinist imprint: it is the image of a Socialism in One Country, enclosed by their own Great Wall.[2]

How fiercely Maoism has been torn by its own contradictions and how the conflict with the Soviet Union has brought its inner tensions to explosion is now evident. The Chinese 'epicentre of revolution' is sending out fresh tremors which shake the whole of Chinese society, touch the Soviet Union, and affect the rest of the world. What are these tremors going to produce? A re-gime which, as the inspirers of the so-called Red Guards prom-ised, would be more egalitarian, less bureaucratic, more directly controlled by the mass of the people, in a word, a regime more socialist than the one under which the Soviet Union has lived? A renascent and purified revolution? Or, was the colossal turmoil we witnessed in 1965-66 only one of those irrational convulsions, typical of bourgeois revolution, when men and parties are unable to control the violent swings of the political pendulum? Were

[2] This was why Mao, cultivating a diplomatic friendship with the govern-ment of General Sokarno for many years encouraged the Indonesian Com-munist Party to accept Sokarno's leadership and to renounce all independent revolutionary action in favour of a coalition with the 'national bourgeoisie.' Mao's role vis-à-vis Indonesian communism was thus very similar to Stalin's role vis-à-vis Chinese communism in the 1920's; and the results have been even more disastrous.

the Red Guards, crowding for month after month the squares and streets of Chinese cities, the new *Enragés* or the Diggers and Levellers of our century? Were they going to win at last? Or did they, when the long paroxysm of utopian fervour and activity was over, drop exhausted, and leave the stage to the high and mighty savior of law and order? Or are perhaps all our historical precedents irrelevant to this drama? Whatever the answer, the conflict between the bourgeois and socialist aspects of the revolution is still unresolved; it goes far deeper than it went in Russia. For one thing, the bourgeois element looms larger in China, represented as it is by the peasantry, which still makes up four-fifths of the nation, and by the numerous and influential survivors of urban capitalism. For another, the anti-bureaucratic and egalitarian momentum of the socialist trend also appears to be greater than it has been in Russia for a very long time. The antagonisms and the collisions, with immense masses of people involved, developed for a time with a stormy spontaneity such as the Soviet Union had not known since its early days—a spontaneity that brings back to one's mind the turbulent crowds of Paris in 1794, in the period of the internecine Jacobin struggles. No matter how this awe-inspiring spectacle ends, and towards what new crossroads it may impel the Soviet Union as well as China, one lesson of these events seems clear: the abolition of man's domination by man can no more be a purely Chinese event than it could be a purely Russian one. It can come about, if at all, only as a truly international event, as a fact of universal history.

VI

Conclusions and Prospects

Coming to the end of this survey of the Soviet half-century we ought to return to the questions with which we began: Has the Russian revolution fulfilled the hopes it has aroused? And what is its significance for our age and generation? I wish I were able to answer the first of these questions with a plain and emphatic yes, and conclude my remarks on a properly triumphal note. Unfortunately, this I cannot do. Yet, a disheartened and pessimistic conclusion would not be justified either. This is still in more than one sense an unfinished revolution. Its record is anything but plain. It is compounded of failure and success, of hope frustrated and hope fulfilled—and who can measure the hopes against one another? Where are the scales on which could be weighed the accomplishments and the frustrations of so great an epoch, and their mutual proportions established? What is evident is the immensity and the unexpected character of both the success and the failure, their interdependence and their glaring contrasts. One is reminded of Hegel's dictum, which has not yet dated, that 'history is not the realm of happiness'; that 'periods of happiness are its empty pages,' for 'although there is no lack of satisfaction in history, satisfaction which comes from the realization of great purposes surpassing any particular in-

97

terest, this is not the same as what is usually described as happiness.' Certainly these fifty years do not belong among history's
empty pages.

'Russia is a big ship destined for big sailing,' this was the poet
Alexander Blok's famous phrase, in which we sense the under-
tone of intense national pride. A Russian looking at the record
of this half-century with the eyes of the nationalist, one who
sees the revolution as a purely Russian event, would have good
reasons to feel even prouder. Russia is now a bigger ship still,
out on a much bigger course. In terms of sheer national power—
and many people the world over still think in these terms—the
balance sheet is to the Soviet Union absolutely satisfactory. Our
statesmen and politicians cannot consider it otherwise than with
envy. Yet it seems to me that few Russians of this generation
contemplate it with undisturbed exultation. Many are conscious
of the fact that October 1917 was not a purely Russian event;
and even those who are not do not necessarily see national power
as history's *ultima ratio*. Most Russians seem aware of the miseries as well as the grandeur of this epoch. They watch the extraordinary impetus of their economic expansion, the rising stacks of
huge and ultra-modern factories, the growing networks of schools
and educational establishments, the feats of Soviet technology,
the space flights, the impressive extension of all social services
and so on; and they have a sense of the vitality and *élan* of
their nation. But they know, too, that for most of them daily
life is still a grinding drudgery, which mocks the splendours of
one of the world's super-Powers.

To give one indication: Despite the immense scale of housing
construction, the average dwelling space per person is still only
six square yards. In view of the prevailing inequality this means
that for many it is only five or four yards, or even less. The
average is still what it was at the end of the Stalin era. This is
not surprising if one recalls that in the last fifteen years alone
the mass of town dwellers has grown by as much as the entire
population of the British Isles. However, such statistics offer

little relief or consolation to people who suffer from the desperate overcrowding; and although the situation is bound to improve gradually, the amelioration will be long in coming. The disproportion between effort and results exemplified by housing is characteristic of many aspects of Soviet life. In all too many fields the Soviet Union has had to run very fast, indeed to engage in a breathless race, only to find that it is still standing in the same place.

Western travellers, struck by the Russians' intense, almost obsessive, preoccupation with material things and with the comforts of life, often speak on this account about the 'Americanization' of the Soviet mentality. Yet the background to this preoccupation is obviously different. In the United States the whole 'way of life' and the dominant ideology encourage the preoccupation with material possessions, while commercial advertising works furiously to excite it constantly so as to induce or sustain artificial consumer demand and prevent overproduction. The Soviet craving for material goods reflects decades of underproduction and underconsumption, weariness with want and privation, and a popular feeling that these can at last be overcome. This popular mood compels the rulers to take greater care than they have been accustomed to take of popular needs and to satisfy them; to this extent it is a progressive factor helping to modernize and civilize the national standard, and 'style,' of living. But as the Soviet way of life is not geared to individual accumulation of wealth, the 'Americanization' is superficial and in all probability characteristic only of the present phase of slow transition from scarcity to abundance.

The spiritual and the political life of the Soviet Union is also variously affected by the grandeur and the miseries of this half-century. Compared with the realm of dread and terror the Soviet Union was, say, fifteen years ago, it is now almost a land of freedom. Gone are the concentration camps of old, whose inmates died like flies, without knowing what they had been punished for. Gone is the all-pervading fear that had atomized the nation, making every man and woman afraid of communicating even with a friend or a relative, and turning the Soviet Union into a country virtually inaccessible to the foreigner. The nation is recovering its mind and speech. The process is slow. It is not easy for people to shed habits they had formed during decades of monolithic discipline. All the same, the change is remarkable. Soviet periodicals are nowadays astir with all sorts of dramatic, though often muffled, controversies; and ordinary people are not greatly inhibited in expressing their genuine political thoughts and feelings to complete strangers, even to tourists from hostile countries, whose inquisitiveness is not always innocuous. Yet the Soviet citizen often frets at the relatively mild bureaucratic tutelage under which he lives as he never fretted at Stalin's despotism. He feels that his spiritual freedom, too, is restricted to something like his miserable six square yards. It is one of the sublime features of the human character that men are not satisfied with what they have achieved, especially when their attainments are dubious or consist of half-gains. Such discontent is the driving force of progress. But it may also become, as it sometimes does in the Soviet Union, a source of frustration and even of sterile cynicism.

In their political life also the Russians all too often feel that they have run fast to keep in the same place. The half-freedom the Soviet Union has won since Stalin's days can indeed be even more excruciating than a complete and hermetic tyranny. Recent Soviet writings, some published in the U.S.S.R., others abroad, have expressed the mortification that arises from this state of affairs, the morose pessimism it sometimes breeds, and even something like the mood of 'Waiting-for-Godot.' But, here again, similarities between Soviet and Western phenomena may be deceptive. The despair which permeates quite a few recent Soviet works of literature is rarely inspired by any metaphysical sense of the 'absurdity of the human condition.' More often than not it expresses, allusively or otherwise, a kind of baffled anger over the outrageous abnormities of Soviet political life, especially over the ambiguities of the official de-Stalinization. The spirit of these writings is more active, satirical, and militant than that which has produced recent Western variations on the old theme of *vanitas vanitatum et vanitas omnia.*

The failure of the official de-Stalinization is at the heart of the malaise. It is more than a decade now since, at the Twentieth Congress, Khrushchev exposed Stalin's misdeeds. That act could make sense only if it had been the prelude to a genuine clarification of the many issues raised by it and to an open nation-wide debate on the legacy of the Stalin era. This has not been the case. Khrushchev and the ruling group at large were eager not to open the debate but to prevent it. They intended the prologue to be also the epilogue of the de-Stalinization. Circumstances compelled them to initiate the process; this had become an imperative necessity of national life. Since the protagonists and even the followers of all anti-Stalinist oppositions had been exterminated, only men of Stalin's entourage were left to inaugurate the de-Stalinization. But the task was uncongenial to them; it went against the grain of their mental habits and interests. They could carry it out only half-heartedly and perfunctorily. They lifted a corner of the curtain over the Stalin era, but could not raise the whole curtain. And so the moral crisis, opened up by Khrushchev's revelations, remains unresolved. His disclosures caused relief and shock, confusion and shame, bewilderment and cynicism. It was a relief for the nation to be freed from the incubus of Stalinism; but it was a shock to realize how heavily the incubus had weighed down the whole body politic. Of course, many a family had suffered from the Stalinist terror and had known it in detail; but only now were they allowed to catch for the first time an over-all glimpse of it, to glance at its true national dimensions. Yet this fleeting glimpse by itself was confusing. And it was a grievous humiliation to be reminded how helplessly the nation had succumbed to the terror, and how meekly it had endured it. Finally, nothing but bewilderment and cynicism could result from the fact

H

that the grim disclosures had been made by Stalin's abettors and accessories, who, having revealed the huge skeleton in their cupboard, at once slammed the door on it and would say no more.

The issue has been too grave and fateful to be treated like this, especially in view of its close bearing on current politics. The official de-Stalinization created new cleavages and aggravated old ones. 'Liberals' and 'radicals,' 'right wing' and 'left wing' communists could not but press for an uninhibited national settling of accounts with the Stalin era and a complete break with it. Crypto-Stalinists, entrenched in the bureaucracy, have been anxious to save as much as possible of the Stalinist method of government and of the Stalin legend. Outside the bureaucracy, especially among the workers, quite a few people have been so antagonized by the hypocrisy of the official de-Stalinization, that they have been almost reconverted to the Stalin cult, or want to hear no more of it and would rather see the whole issue buried once and for all.

At the back of the divisions there is the fact that Soviet society does not know itself and is intensely conscious of this. The history of this half-century is a closed book even to the Soviet intelligentsia. Like someone who had long been struck with amnesia and only begins to recover, the nation not knowing its recent past does not understand its present. Decades of Stalinist falsification have induced the collective amnesia; and the half-truths with which the Twentieth Congress initiated the process of recovery are blocking its progress. But sooner or later the Soviet Union must take stock of this half-century, if its political consciousness is ᴛo develop and crystallize in new and positive forms.

This is a situation of especial interest to historians and political theorists; it offers a rare, perhaps a unique, example of the close interdependence of history, politics, and social consciousness. Historians often argue whether an awareness of the past contributes at all to the wisdom of statesmen and to the political intelligence of ordinary people. Some believe it does; others take the view Heine once expressed in the aphorism that history teaches us that it teaches nothing. In class society political thinking, governed by class or group interest, benefits from the study of the past only within the limits required or permitted by interest. Even the historian's views are conditioned by social background and political circumstances. Normally, 'the ideas of the ruling class' tend to be 'the ruling ideas of an epoch.' In some epochs those ideas favour a more or less objective study of history, and political thinking gains thereby; in others they act as powerful inhibiting factors. Whatever the case, no ruling group and no society, if it is only a little more than half-civilized, can function without possessing some form of historical consciousness satisfactory to itself, without a consciousness giving most members of the ruling group and of society at large the conviction that their view of the past, especially of the recent past, is not just a tissue of falsehoods, but that it corresponds to real facts and occurrences. No ruling group can live by cynicism alone. Statesmen, leaders, and ordinary people alike need to have the subjective feeling that what they stand for is morally right; and what is morally right cannot rest on historical distortions or forgeries. And although distortions and even plain forgeries have entered into the thinking of every nation, their very effectiveness depends on whether the nation concerned accepts them as truth.

In the Soviet Union the moral crisis of the post-Stalin years consists of a profound disturbance of the nation's historical and political consciousness. Since the Twentieth Congress, people have been aware how much of what they once believed was made up of forgeries and myths. They want to learn the truth but are denied access to it. Their rulers have told them that virtually the whole record of the revolution has been falsified; but they have not thrown open the true record. To give again only a few instances: the last great scandal of the Stalin era, the so-called Doctors' Plot, has been officially denounced on the ground that the plot was a concoction. But whose concoction was it? Was Stalin alone responsible for it? And what purpose was it to serve? These questions are still unanswered. Khrushchev has suggested that the Soviet Union might not have suffered the huge losses inflicted on it in the last war had it not been for Stalin's errors and miscalculations. Yet those 'errors' have not become the subject of an open debate. The Nazi-Soviet Pact of 1939 is, officially, still taboo. The people have been told about the horrors of the concentration camps and about the frame-ups and forced confessions by means of which the Great Purges had been staged. But the victims of the Purges, apart from a few exceptions, have not been rehabilitated. No one knows just how many people were deported to the camps; how many died; how many were massacred; and how many survived. A similar conspiracy of silence surrounds the circumstances of the forcible collectivization. Every one of these questions has been raised; none has been answered. Even in this jubilee year most of the leaders of 1917 remain 'unpersons'; the names of most members of the Central Committee who directed the October rising are still unmentionable. People are asked to celebrate the great anniversary, but they cannot read a single trustworthy account of the events they are celebrating. (Nor can they get hold of any history of the civil war.) The ideological edifice of Stalinism has been exploded; but, with its foundations shattered, its roof blown off, and its walls charred and threatening to come down with a crash, the structure still stands; and the people are required to live in it.

Opening this series of lectures I alluded to the blessings and curses of the continuity of the Soviet regime. We have dwelt on the blessings; now we see the curses as well. Sheltered by continuity, the irrational aspects of the revolution survive and endure together with the rational ones. Can they be separated from one another? It is clearly in the Soviet Union's vital interest that it should overcome the irrationalities and release its creative powers from their grip. The present incongruous combination breeds intense disillusionment; and because of this the miseries of the revolution may, in the eyes of the people, come to over-shadow its grandeur. When this happened in past revolutions the result was restoration. But although restoration was a tre-mendous setback, indeed a tragedy, to the nation that succumbed to it, it had its redeeming feature: it demonstrated to a people disillusioned with the revolution how inacceptable the reaction-ary alternative was. Returned Bourbons and Stuarts taught the people much better than Puritans, Jacobins, or Bonapartists could, that there was no way back to the past; that the basic work of the revolution was irreversible; and that it must be saved for the future. Unwittingly, the restoration thus rehabilitated the revolution, or at least its essential and rational accom-plishments.

In the Soviet Union, we know, the revolution has survived all possible agents of restoration. Yet it seems to be burdened with a mass of accumulated disillusionment and even despair that in other historical circumstances might have been the driving force of a restoration. At times the Soviet Union appears to be fraught with the moral-psychological potentiality of restoration that can-not become a political actuality. Much of the record of these fifty years is utterly discredited in the eyes of the people; and no returned Romanovs are going to rehabilitate it. The revolution must rehabilitate itself, by its own efforts.

Soviet society cannot reconcile itself for much longer to re-maining a mere object of history and being dependent on the whims of autocrats or the arbitrary decisions of oligarchies. It needs to regain the sense of being its own master. It needs to obtain control over its governments and to transform the State, which has so long towered above society, into an instrument of the nation's democratically expressed will and interest. It needs, in the first instance, to re-establish freedom of expression and association. This is a modest aspiration compared with the ideal of a classless and stateless society; and it is paradoxical that the Soviet people should now have to strive for those elementary liberties which once figured in all bourgeois liberal programmes, programmes which Marxism rightly subjected to its ruthless criticism.

In a post-capitalist society, however, freedom of expression and association has to perform a function radically different from that which it has performed in capitalism. It need hardly be stressed here how essential that freedom has been to progress even under capitalism. Yet, in bourgeois society it can be a formal freedom only. Prevailing property relations render it so, for the possessing classes exercise an almost monopolistic control over nearly all the means of opinion formation. The working classes and their intellectual mouthpieces manage to get hold of, at best, marginal facilities for social and political self-expression. Society, being itself controlled by property, cannot effectively control the State. All the more generously is it allowed to indulge in the illusion that it does so, unless keeping up the illusion causes the bourgeoisie too much embarrassment and expense.ᐧ In a society like the Soviet, freedom of expression and association cannot have so formal and illusory a character: either it is real, or it does not exist at all. The power of property having been destroyed, only the State, that is, the bureaucracy, dominates society; and its domination is based solely on the suppression of the people's liberty to criticize and oppose. Capitalism could afford to enfranchise the working classes, for it could rely on its economic mechanism to keep them in subjection; the bourgeoisie maintains its social preponderance even when it exercises no political power. In post-capitalist society no automatic economic mechanism keeps the masses in subjection; it is sheer political force that does it. True, the bureaucracy derives part of its strength from the uncontrolled commanding position it holds in the economy; but it holds that too by means of political force. Without that force it cannot maintain its social supremacy; and any form of democratic control deprives it of its force. Hence the new meaning and function of the freedom of expression and association. In other words, capitalism has been

able to battle against its class enemies from many economic, political, and cultural lines of defence, with much scope for re-
treat and maneouvre. A post-capitalist bureaucratic dictatorship
has far less scope: its first, its political line of defence, is its last.
No wonder that it holds that line with all the tenacity it can
muster.

The post-capitalist relationship between State and society is
far less simple, however, than some ultra-radical critics imagine.
There can, in my view, be no question of any so-called abolition
of bureaucracy. Bureaucracy, like the State itself, cannot be
simply obliterated. The existence of expert and professional
groups of civil servants, administrators, and managers is part and
parcel of a necessary social division of labour which reflects wide
discrepancies and cleavages between various skills and degrees of
education, between skilled and unskilled labour, and, more
fundamentally, between brain and brawn. These discrepancies
and cleavages are diminishing; and their reduction foreshadows
a time when they may become socially so insignificant that State
and bureaucracy may indeed wither away. But this is still a relatively remote prospect. What seems possible in the near future
is that society should be able to retrieve its civil liberties and establish political control over the State. In striving for this the
Soviet people are not just re-enacting one of the old battles that
bourgeois liberalism had fought against absolutism; they are
rather following up their own great struggle of 1917.

The outcome will, of course, greatly depend on events in the
outside world. The tremendous, and to us still obscure, upheaval
in China must affect the Soviet Union as well. In so far as it
loosens up or upsets one post-revolutionary bureaucratic-mono-
lithic structure and releases popular forces, rising from the depth
of society, for spontaneous political action, the Chinese example
may stimulate similar processes across the Soviet border. China
is undoubtedly in some respects more progressive than the Soviet Union, if only because she was able to learn from Russia's
experience and avoid some of the latter's erratic drifts and blun-

ders; and she has been less affected by bureaucratic ossification. On the other hand, China's economic and social structure is primitive and backward; and Maoism carries, in its rituals and cults, the dead weight of that backwardness. Consequently, the lessons it sets out to teach the world have all too often little or no relevance to the problems of more highly developed societies; and even when Maoism has something positive to offer, it usually does it in so rigidly orthodox a manner and in such archaic forms that the positive content is all too easily overlooked. And when the Maoists try to galvanize the Stalinist cult, they merely shock and antagonize all forward-looking elements in the U.S.S.R. But perhaps the Russo-Chinese conflict may drive home one important lesson, namely, that arrogant bureaucratic oligarchies, incorrigible in their national narrow-mindedness and egoism, cannot be expected to work out any rational solution of this or any other conflict; still less can they lay stable foundations for a socialist commonwealth of peoples.

Events in the West will contribute even more decisively, for good or evil, to the further internal evolution of the Soviet Union. We may leave aside here the frequently discussed and more obvious, diplomatic and military aspects of the problem: it is evident enough what severe restrictions the cold war and the international arms race place on the growth of welfare and the enlargement of liberty in the U.S.S.R. More fundamental and difficult is the issue of the stalemate in the class struggle, the makings of which were examined earlier. Is this stalemate going to last? Or is it only a fleeting moment of equilibrium? The view that it is going to last has gained much ground recently among Western political theorists and historians; many are inclined to consider it as the final outcome of the contest between capitalism and socialism. (No doubt this opinion has its adherents in the Soviet Union and Eastern Europe as well.) The argument is conducted on various social-economic and historical levels.

The social structures of the U.S.S.R. and the U.S.A., it is

pointed out, have, from their opposite starting points, evolved and moved towards one another so closely that their differences are increasingly irrelevant and the similarities are decisive. Among others, Professor John Kenneth Galbraith expounds this idea in his Reith Lectures. He speaks emphatically about the 'convergence of structure in countries with advanced industrial organization' and surveys the main points of the convergence in American society. There is the supremacy of the managerial elements; the divorce of management from ownership; the continuous concentration of industrial power and the extension of the scales of its operation; the withering away of *laissez faire* and of the market; the growing economic role of the State; and, consequently, the inescapable necessity of planning, which is needed not merely to prevent slumps and depressions, but to maintain normal social efficiency. 'We have seen,' says Professor Galbraith, 'that industrial technology has an imperative that transcends ideology.' Pricking some current Western misconceptions about 'the revival of a market economy in the U.S.S.R.,' Professor Galbraith remarks: 'There is no tendency for the Soviet and the Western systems to convergence by the return of the Soviet system to the market. Both have outgrown that. What exists is a perceptible and very important convergence to the same form of planning under the growing authority of the business firm.' In this presentation the 'convergence' appears to occur not so much halfway between the two systems, as just within the boundaries of socialism, and the picture is not one of stalemate, but rather of a diagonal resulting from the parallelogram of capitalist and socialist pressures.[1]

Historians find a precedent for this situation in the struggle between Reformation and Counter-Reformation. Professor Butterfield, one of the early exponents of this analogy, points out that at the outset of their conflict both Protestantism and

---

[1] The quotations are from Professor Galbraith's Reith Lectures as published in *The Listener* (15 December 1966).

Catholicism aspired to total victory; but that, having reached a deadlock, they were compelled to seek mutual accommodation, to 'co-exist peacefully' and content themselves with their respective 'zones of influence' in Western Christianity.[2] In the meantime, their initial ideological antagonism had been whittled down by a process of mutual assimilation: the Church of Rome enhanced its strength by absorbing elements of Protestantism; while Protestantism, growing dogmatic and sectarian, lost much of its attraction and came to resemble its adversary. The stalemate was thus unbreakable and final; so is the deadlock between the opposed ideologies of our time—on this point the arguments of our historians and of the political or economic theorists converge.

The historical analogy, convincing though it is in some points, has its faults and flaws. As such analogies often do, it overlooks basic differences between historic epochs. In the age of the Reformation, Western society was fragmented into a multitude of feudal, semi-feudal, post-feudal, pre-capitalist, and early capitalist principalities. The Protestant consciousness played its prominent part in the formation of the nation-state; but the nation-state set the outer limits to its unifying tendencies. The reunification of Western Christianity under the aegis of one Church was an historic impossibility. In contrast to this, the technological basis of modern society, its structure and its conflicts, are international or even universal in character; they tend towards international or universal solutions. And there are the unprecedented dangers threatening our biological existence. These, above all, press for the unification of mankind, which cannot be achieved without an integrating principle of social organization.

Protestantism and Catholicism confronted one another pri-

[2] H. Butterfield, *International Conflict in the Twentieth Century, A Christian View* (London 1960), pp. 61-78. My criticism of Professor Butterfield's analogy does not detract from the soundness of his courageous pleas for an international *détente* which he addressed to American audiences in the 1950s.

marily in ideological terms; but in the background there was the great conflict between rising capitalism and declining feudalism. This was by no means brought to a halt by the ideological-religious stalemate. The division of spheres between Reformation and Counter-Reformation corresponded, very broadly, to a division between the two social systems and to a temporary equilibrium between them. As the contest between the feudal and the bourgeois ways of life went on, it assumed new ideological forms. The more mature bourgeois consciousness of the eighteenth century expressed itself not in religious but in secularist ideologies, philosophical and political. The stalemate between Protestantism and Catholicism was perpetuated on a margin of history, as it were; for all practical historical purposes, in effective social and political action, it was transcended. Not only did the social conflict not congeal with the religious divisions, but it was fought out to the end. After all, capitalism achieved total victory in Europe. It did so by a wide variety of means and methods, by revolutions from below and revolutions from above, and after many temporary deadlocks and partial defeats. Thus even in the terms of this analogy it seems at least premature to conclude that the present ideological stalemate between East and West brings to a close the historic confrontation between capitalism and socialism. The forms and ideological expressions of the antagonism may and must vary; but it does not follow that the momentum of the conflict is spent or diminished. Incidentally, the story of the Reformation offers many a warning against hasty conclusions about ideological deadlocks. When one is told that a hundred and twenty years have passed since the *Communist Manifesto* without a victorious socialist revolution in the West, one thinks willy-nilly of the many 'premature' starts the Reformation made and of the protracted manner in which its ideology and movement took shape. More than a century lay between Hus and Luther; and yet another century separated Luther from the Puritan revolution.

But has not the Marxist analysis of society, and have not the universal aspirations of the Russian revolution, been invalidated by the mutual assimilation of the opposed social systems? A degree of assimilation is undeniable; and it is due to the supranational levelling impact of modern technology and to the logic of any major confrontation which imposes identical or similar methods of action on the contestants. The changes in the structure of Western, especially American, society are striking indeed. But when we look at them closely, what do we see? The deepening divorce of management from property, the importance of the managerial elements, the concentration of capital, the ever more elaborate division of labour within any huge corporation and between the corporations; the withering away of the market and *laissez faire*; the increase in the economic weight of the State; and the technological and the economic necessity of planning—all these are in fact manifestations of that socialization of the productive process which, according to Marxism, develops in capitalism. Indeed the socialization has now been immensely accelerated. In the description of the process which Marx gave in *Das Kapital*, he very clearly foreshadowed precisely these developments and trends that seem so novel and revolutionary to Western analysts. Has not Professor Galbraith described to us something with which we are, or should be, familiar, namely, the rapid growth of the 'embryo of socialism within the womb of capitalism'? The embryo is evidently getting bigger and bigger. Should we therefore conclude that there is no longer any need for the act of birth? The Marxist will reflect over the paradox that while in Russia the midwife of revolution intervened before the embryo had had the time to mature, in the West the embryo may well have grown over-mature; and the consequences may become extremely dangerous to the social organism.

The fact is that, regardless of all Keynesian innovations, our productive process, so magnificently socialized in many respects, is not yet socially controlled. Property, no matter how much it is divorced from management, still controls the economy. The shareholder's profit is still its regulating motive, subject only to the needs of militarism and of the world-wide struggle against communism. In any case, our economy and social existence remain anarchic and irrational. The anarchy may not show itself in periodic deep slumps and depressions, although, on a longer view, even this is not certain. European capitalism, within its smaller compass, knew, after the Franco-Prussian war of 1870, a similar and even more prolonged prosperity, undisturbed by deep slumps; and this led Edward Bernstein and his fellow revisionists to conclude that events had given the lie to the Marxist analysis and prognostication. Soon thereafter, however, the economy was shaken by convulsions more violent than ever, and mankind was ushered into the epoch of world wars and revolutions.

Nothing would be more welcome, especially to the Marxist, than the knowledge that capitalist property relations have become so irrelevant in Western society that they no longer hinder it in organizing rationally its productive forces and creative powers. Yet the test of this is whether our society can control and marshal its resources and energies for constructive purposes and for its own general welfare; and whether it can organize and plan them internationally as well as nationally. Until now our society has failed this test. Our governments have forestalled slumps and depressions by planning for destruction and death rather than for life and welfare. Not for nothing do our economists, financial experts, and jobbers speculate gloomily on what would happen to the Western economy if, for instance, the American Administration were not to spend nearly 80 billion dollars on armament in one year. Among all the dark images of declining capitalism ever drawn by Marxists, not a single one was as black and apocalyptic as the picture that reality is producing. About sixty years ago Rosa Luxemburg predicted that one day militarism would become *the* driving force of the capitalist economy; but even her forecast pales before the facts.

This is why the message of 1917 remains valid for the world at large. The present ideological deadlock and the social status quo can hardly serve as the basis either for the solution of the problems of our epoch or even for mankind's survival. Of course, it would be the ultimate disaster if the nuclear super-Powers were to treat the social status quo as their plaything and if either of them tried to alter it by force of arms. In this sense the peaceful co-existence of East and West is a paramount historic necessity. But the social status quo cannot be perpetuated. Karl Marx speaking about stalemates in past class struggles notes that they usually ended 'in the common ruin of the contending classes.' A stalemate indefinitely prolonged, and guaranteed by a perpetual balance of nuclear deterrents, is sure to lead the contending classes and nations to their common and ultimate ruin. Humanity needs unity for its sheer survival; where can it find it if not in socialism? And great though the Russian and the Chinese revolutions loom in the perspective of our century, Western initiative is still essential for the further progress of socialism.

Hegel once remarked that 'world history moves from the East to the West' and that 'Europe represents the close of world history,' whereas Asia was only its beginning. This arrogant view was inspired by Hegel's belief that the Reformation and the Prussian State were the culmination of mankind's spiritual development; yet many people in the West, worshippers of neither State nor Church, believed until recently that world history had indeed found its final abode in the West, and that the East, having nothing significant to contribute, could only be its object. We know better. We have seen how vigorously history has moved back to the East. However, we need not assume that it ends there and that the West will forever go on speaking in its present conservative voice and contribute to the annals of socialism only a few more empty pages. Socialism has still some decisive revolutionary acts to perform in the West as well as in the East; and nowhere will history come to a close. The East has been the first to give effect to the great principle of a new social organization, the principle originally conceived in the West.

Fifty years of Soviet history tell us what stupendous progress a backward nation has achieved by applying that principle, even in the most adverse conditions. By this alone these years point to the limitless new horizons that Western society can open to itself and to the world if only it frees itself from its conservative fetishes. In this sense the Russian revolution still confronts the West with a grave and challenging *tua res agitur*.